The GREATEST MOMENTS in SPORTS

by Len Berman

SOURCEBOOKS
Jabberwocky™
AN IMPRINT OF SOURCEBOOKS

To my dad, Syde, for passing along his writing genes, and to my mom, "Grammar" Helen, who has always helped me to get it right.

Published by Sourcebooks Jabberwocky, an imprint of Sourcebooks, Inc.

P.O. Box 4410, Naperville, Illinois 60567-4410

(630) 961-3900

Fax: (630) 961-2168

www.jabberwockykids.com

Library of Congress Cataloging-in-Publication Data

Berman, Len.

The greatest moments in sports / Len Berman.

p. cm.

1. Sports—History. 2. Sports—Miscellanea. I. Title.

GV576.B44 2009

796—dc22

2009023686

Printed by: O.G. Printing Productions, Ltd., Kowloon, Hong Kong

ID # 12105

03/10

Printed and bound in China

OGP 10 9 8 7 6 5 4 3

CONTENTS

INTRODUCTION

What were the greatest moments in sports history? Ask 25 sports fans, and you may get 25 different answers. For example, you might think the invention of baseball would make the list. Good thought. But the funny thing is historians can't even agree who actually invented the game. Some say it was Abner Doubleday, who was a general in the Civil War! Others say the real inventor was a guy named Alexander Cartwright. He lived in New York in the mid-1850s.

So, if they can't even agree on who thought up America's pastime, then who can really say what the greatest moments in sports history were? Well, for one, I can! I've seen a few sports events in my day: lots of World Series, Super Bowls, and Olympics. You may or may not agree with my choices, but for each moment, I'll tell you why I thought it was one of the greatest. It could be the drama of the moment. Perhaps it was historical or just plain amazing. But in every case, the moment is great. And we've included a CD so you can hear some of these incredible moments as they were broadcast live. Watch for this icon throughout the book. ⟶

LISTEN *to this* **MOMENT TRACK 1**

So, don't stay up tonight worrying about who really invented baseball. It doesn't matter. What really counts is the number of amazing moments that have happened in that sport. By my count, five of the greatest moments in sports happened in baseball. See if you agree. At the end of the book, I'll give you a chance to tell me what you think. By the way, the moments in this book are presented in no particular order, but I do have a strong opinion for which is the number one all-time greatest sports moment, so read on!

MICHAEL

PHELPS

There is an old saying in sports that "records are made to be broken." But that's not always true. There are some records that may never be broken. One that comes to mind is the New York Yankees Joe DiMaggio. He got at least one base hit in 56 consecutive games in 1941. Maybe someday someone will come along and get a hit in 57 consecutive games, but it seems unlikely. Here's another one. In 1938, Cincinnati Reds pitcher Johnny Vander Meer pitched two consecutive no-hitters! To break his record, a Major League Baseball pitcher would have to throw three straight no-hit games. Trust me. That's not going to happen. At the 1972 Olympics in Munich, Germany, American swimmer Mark Spitz won seven gold medals. It was so unbelievable that most experts said it would never happen again. But it did in 2008.

Michael Phelps was born in Baltimore in 1985. Things weren't so great for him as a kid. When he was nine, his parents got divorced. In addition to that, doctors said he had something called ADHD. He had trouble paying attention. He had so much extra energy, he couldn't sit still. At first, he had to take medication to help him concentrate. But he also tried something else: swimming! He was able to burn off all that extra energy in the pool. And I'd say he got pretty good at the sport. In fact, he was so good that at the age of 15, Michael was the youngest male in 68 years to make the U.S. Olympic swim team. At the 2000 Olympics in Sydney, Australia, he swam the 200-meter butterfly and finished in fifth place. Not bad for the teenager. But just wait!

Along came the Athens, Greece, Olympics in 2004. He was now 19 years old and went from a fifth-place finish in one event in 2000 to swimming in eight events. Michael won six gold medals and two bronzes—the second-greatest swimming Olympics that anyone had ever had. Spitz's record was safe for now. But just wait!

Mark Spitz wears his seven gold medals from the 1972 Olympics.

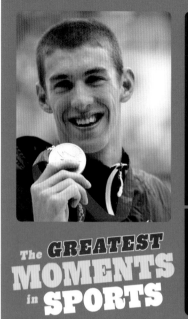

MICHAEL PHELPS

BORN: June 30, 1985

BIRTHPLACE: Baltimore, Maryland

HEIGHT: 6'4"   **WEIGHT:** 185 lbs.

TEAM: U.S. Olympic Swim Team

SPECIALTIES: Freestyle, Butterfly, Backstroke, Breaststroke

FAST FACT: Michael has won a total of 16 Olympic medals (14 gold and 2 bronze).

The **GREATEST MOMENTS** *in* **SPORTS**

The Opening Ceremony for the 2008 Olympics in Beijing, China, began at eight minutes after eight in the evening on August 8, 2008. In other words, 8:08 on 8/8/08. Eight is a lucky number in China. It was also the number of finals that Michael, now 23, planned to swim. So, if he could somehow win them all, he'd win an astounding eight gold medals, one more than Spitz did in Munich.

At the Olympics, you have to qualify before you can swim in the finals. This meant that if Michael were to swim in eight finals, he would actually have to swim 17 different races over a nine-day period against the best swimmers in the world. And it wasn't as if he was swimming eight races

individually. Only five would be by himself. Three of the finals would be relays, meaning he had three teammates in each of those races. If any one of the other guys had a bad day, it would doom Michael and ruin his chance to make history. In short, Michael was trying to do the unthinkable.

The first of Michael's 17 races came at the Water Cube (the swimming center in Beijing) the night after the Opening Ceremony. That evening, he would race in a qualifying heat for the 400-meter individual medley.

Twenty-nine swimmers competed in four different heats to choose the eight best for the final. Michael not only swam the fastest time in his heat, but he was the fastest of all 29 trying to qualify. The eight swimmers who made it to the final didn't have long to wait. The first swimming final of the 2008 Olympics would be held in about 13 hours, at 8 a.m. on Sunday. This was the first chance for Michael to win the gold medal.

Michael went into the race as the favorite. He was the world-record holder in this event. And he didn't disappoint. Michael not only won the race, but he also broke his own world record by more than a second. Gold medal number one. World record number one. But could he relax the rest of that day? No way. Later that night, he had to swim again in a qualifying heat for the 200-meter freestyle. He finished second in his heat, but he was fast enough to qualify for the semifinals. Now his day was done. One gold medal down; seven to go.

The next day was even crazier. At ten o'clock in the morning, he swam in the semifinals of the 200-meter freestyle and qualified for the finals the next morning. And then about 80 minutes later, he had to get into the water for the final of the 4x100-meter freestyle. What sports fans around the world were about to see would be one of the most exciting moments of the entire Olympics.

Remember, Michael had to depend on three teammates to accomplish his golden goals. Michael swam the first 100 meters. Not bad. He broke the American record, but his time was only good enough for second place to the Australians. Michael then stood on the pool deck and became the most famous cheerleader in swimming history.

With just one length of the pool left, the Americans were trailing the French. And then the fourth American swimmer, Jason Lezak, went to work. With Michael cheering him on, Lezak swam the fastest 100 meters in relay history. It came down to the final stroke. Lezak and Alain Bernard of France both reached for the wall, and Lezak touched first by an incredible eight one-hundredths of a second!

Garrett Weber-Gale and Michael Phelps celebrate as their team wins the gold in the 4x100–meter freestyle relay.

In a medley, you swim two lengths of the pool in the butterfly, then two lengths backstroke, two lengths breaststroke, and finally two lengths freestyle. *Freestyle* means you can swim any stroke you want, but everyone does the crawl because it's the fastest.

The United States had won! Two golds for Michael. Two world records. But this one would have been impossible without a little help from his friends.

The next several days were a blur. Michael won gold medal after gold medal. He swam heats, finishing first

TEAMWORK!

Three of Michael's gold medals were the result of some serious teamwork. These teammates helped Michael make history!

Michael Phelps   Brendan Hansen   Jason Lezak   Aaron Peirsol

4x100 M FREESTYLE RELAY

Garrett Weber-Gale

Cullen Jones

Jason Lezak

4x200 M FREESTYLE RELAY

Ryan Lochte

Ricky Berens

Peter Vanderkaay

4x100 M MEDLEY

Aaron Peirsol

Brendan Hansen

Jason Lezak

or second every time. One day, he won two gold medals an hour apart and set world records in both! And that same night, he finished first in another heat. It was wild. Michael said: "I eat, sleep, and swim. That's all I do." We don't know much about the sleeping, but the other stuff was unbelievable. Along the way, he won his fourth gold medal, which, when added to his six from Athens, totaled 10! Nobody in Olympic history had ever won 10 gold medals.

As dawn broke in Beijing on Saturday, August 16, 2008, here's what Michael had done so far: He had now swum 15 heats and finals. He had qualified in every heat, and in all six finals that he raced, he had won a gold medal *and* set a world record. He was still one gold medal shy of Spitz's record of seven. Nobody could have predicted what was about to happen.

That morning was the final of the 100-meter butterfly (two lengths of the pool). Michael was trying to "tie history." Halfway through the race, Michael was in seventh place. Would this be the race he would finally lose? One by one, Michael started catching up to the other competitors when, at last, only a Serbian swimmer, Milorad Čavić, stood between Michael and gold. But Čavić wouldn't fade. The two of them splashed to the finish and then it was over.

Everyone in the Water Cube thought Michael lost. On television, Michael's mom was holding up two fingers:

second place. But wait! The scoreboard flashed a "1" next to Michael's name. How was that possible? Did he actually win? Officials slowed down the tape of the finish as slow as they could. There was Čavić with his two arms outstretched gliding to the wall. And there was Michael taking one more "half stroke." The instant before Čavić could hit the wall, Michael's long arms came crashing down, hitting the wall first! The margin of victory was the smallest you can possibly have—just one one-hundredth of a second. On television, the announcers screamed that it was magical. Everywhere else, they were calling it a miracle. Whatever you called it, Michael had done it. His seventh gold medal, tying the all-time record for one Olympics.

There was still one more race to swim. The next morning was the 4x100 medley relay. Michael swam third and did the butterfly. Of course, he gave the United States the lead. Of course, they won the gold. Of course, it was another world record. And now he had done it—the unthinkable—eight gold medals in one Olympics!

And so, the final totals for Michael: eight finals, seven world records (the eighth was an Olympic record), and most of all those record-setting eight gold medals. And when you add the six he won in Athens in 2004, it totaled 14! That's five more than anyone had ever won before.

The kid from Baltimore who once had trouble paying attention had the entire world paying attention to him.

MICHAEL'S BREAKFAST:

- a large bowl of hot cereal
- three fried-egg sandwiches
- a huge omelet
- french toast
- pancakes topped with chocolate chips
- two cups of coffee

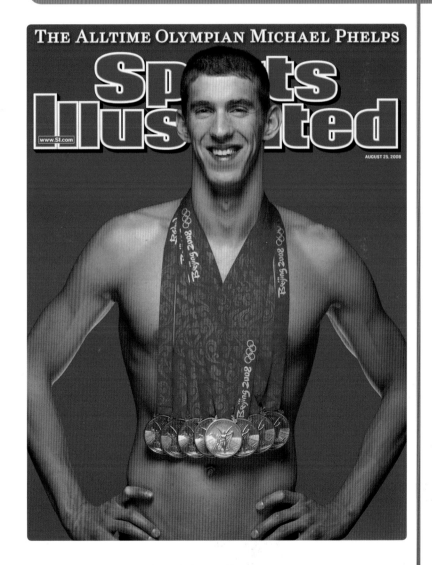

THE ALLTIME OLYMPIAN MICHAEL PHELPS
Sports Illustrated
www.SI.com
AUGUST 25, 2008

THE BABE'S CALLED SHOT

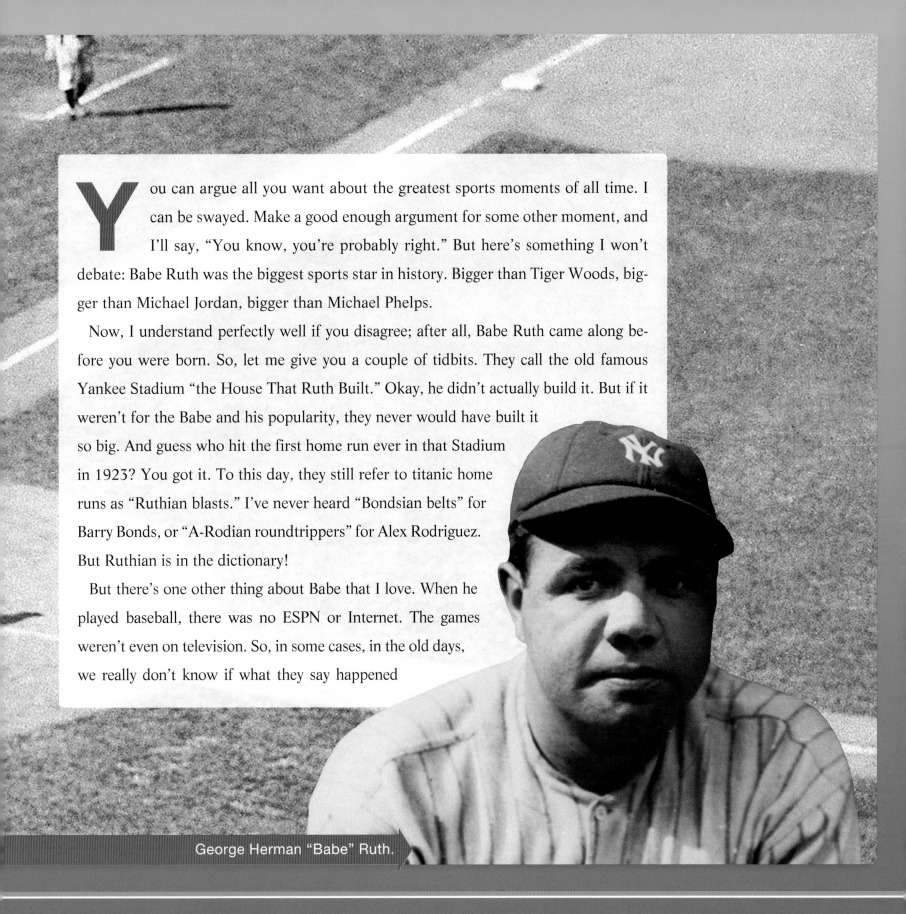

You can argue all you want about the greatest sports moments of all time. I can be swayed. Make a good enough argument for some other moment, and I'll say, "You know, you're probably right." But here's something I won't debate: Babe Ruth was the biggest sports star in history. Bigger than Tiger Woods, bigger than Michael Jordan, bigger than Michael Phelps.

Now, I understand perfectly well if you disagree; after all, Babe Ruth came along before you were born. So, let me give you a couple of tidbits. They call the old famous Yankee Stadium "the House That Ruth Built." Okay, he didn't actually build it. But if it weren't for the Babe and his popularity, they never would have built it so big. And guess who hit the first home run ever in that Stadium in 1923? You got it. To this day, they still refer to titanic home runs as "Ruthian blasts." I've never heard "Bondsian belts" for Barry Bonds, or "A-Rodian roundtrippers" for Alex Rodriguez. But Ruthian is in the dictionary!

But there's one other thing about Babe that I love. When he played baseball, there was no ESPN or Internet. The games weren't even on television. So, in some cases, in the old days, we really don't know if what they say happened

George Herman "Babe" Ruth.

This is the House That Ruth Built— also known as the old Yankee Stadium.

George Herman Ruth Jr. had some of the best nicknames in sports history, including: the **GREAT BAMBINO**, the **SULTAN OF SWAT**, and (of course) the **BABE**!

really happened. And that leads us right to the 1932 World Series. I can guarantee you that the other greatest moments in this book actually occurred. But what happened on October 1, 1932, has been talked and speculated about forever.

The 1932 World Series was between Ruth's New York Yankees and the Chicago Cubs. There were a bunch of things on Ruth's mind. He had a fabulous year, even though he was getting older and had gained a lot of weight. (He was now 37, and he was never skinny.) It was thought his game was slowing down. He batted .341 that year, hit 41 home runs, and knocked in 137 runs. A fabulous season for any ballplayer. But by Ruthian standards, those numbers were all lower than the year before. Ruth was out to prove that his critics were wrong. He was still "the Babe."

On top of that, the Yankees didn't like the Cubs for a couple of reasons. The Yankees manager was Joe McCarthy. He had been the Cubs manager, but Chicago had fired him even though he led them to the pennant in 1929. And there was one more reason. Mark Koenig was the shortstop on the 1927 Yankee team that people called "Murderers' Row." Koenig had been with the Yankees for six years, but in 1932, he joined the Cubs and helped them win the pennant.

Here's where money comes into the story. Baseball teams are paid a bonus for winning the pennant. The players then vote to see how they divide up the loot. When the Cubs won the 1932 pennant, the players voted that Koenig should get half as much money as everyone else. After all, he had only been with them part of the season. Well, Koenig was Babe's buddy, so Babe Ruth thought the Cubs were cheapskates. With all that stuff swirling around, the World Series began.

The first two games were at Yankee Stadium. Ruth didn't hit any homers, but he got on base five times and

In the 1930s, the average price for a ticket to see a baseball game was only a little more than a dollar.

Babe Ruth always hit with power.

GEORGE HERMAN "BABE" RUTH JR.

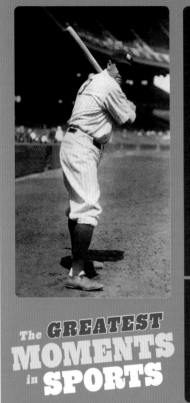

BORN: February 6, 1895

BIRTHPLACE: Baltimore, Maryland

HEIGHT: 6'2" **WEIGHT:** 215 lbs.

TEAM: Boston Red Sox (1914–1919), NY Yankees (1920–1934)

BATTED: Left **THREW:** Left

POSITIONS: Pitcher, Right Field, First Base

NUMBER: 3

FAST FACT: Babe was not only one of the greatest home run sluggers of all time, but he was also a talented pitcher.

The GREATEST MOMENTS in SPORTS

THE BABY RUTH CANDY BAR:

It was probably named after Babe Ruth in 1921. The candy company claimed it was named after President Grover Cleveland's daughter Ruth, but Cleveland had left the White House years earlier.

scored four runs. The Yankees easily won both games. And now the scene shifted to Wrigley Field in Chicago for Game 3 and that fateful day.

The Cubs players knew what Ruth thought of them, and they called him all sorts of names. How did the Babe respond? In the first inning, he stepped to the plate with two men on base and promptly hit a three-run homer! Just like that, the Yankees were rolling, with Babe Ruth leading the way. When Ruth went out to play right field for the bottom of the first inning, the crowd booed him and threw lemons in his direction. But Ruth wasn't bothered. He simply tipped his cap and smiled to the crowd.

When Babe Ruth came to bat in the fifth inning, the score was tied 4–4. Another lemon was thrown from the stands, and it rolled near home plate. The Cubs players in the dugout were yelling all sorts of nasty stuff at the Babe. Charlie Root was the pitcher, and the count was two balls and two strikes.

Everything I've said so far is fact. But what happened next is the stuff of legend.

Before the next pitch, Babe Ruth pointed. Was he pointing at the center-field bleachers and predicting that he was going to hit a home run? Maybe. Perhaps he was pointing at Root or maybe at the Cubs dugout as if to say, "I'll show you." No one knows for sure what he was pointing at, but just about everyone agrees that he definitely pointed. And the very next pitch—boom! A titanic home run to center field. The longest homer they had ever seen at Wrigley Field.

Babe Ruth had given the Yankees the lead for good. And as he rounded the bases, he waved at the Cubs dugout as if to say: "Take that. I told you so." Wrigley Field was in an uproar, and right in the middle of it, as always, was the Babe.

Root must have been rattled. The next pitch was to Lou Gehrig, and he also hit a homer! The Cubs never recovered and lost the game 7–5. The next day, the Yankees easily won 13–6, sweeping the World Series in four straight games.

"The Babe's Called Shot" was his last World Series hit and his 15th and last World Series homer. Because Babe Ruth loved the attention, he never denied that he had pointed to the center-field bleachers. If people thought that he had predicted his titanic blast, then that was just fine with him.

While the game wasn't on television (TV hadn't been invented yet), there are some films of the game. And guess what? The films show him pointing at *something*. What it was, well, I guess we'll never really know. I do know one thing. Whether it really happened or not, it was one of the greatest moments in sports history.

Babe Ruth shares stories of his life with young fans.

Babe Ruth loved children and even asked one lucky kid to be his personal mascot! Ray Kelly was three years old when the Babe saw him and his dad playing catch in the park. Little Ray got to wear a matching Yankees uniform and sit in the dugout with Ruth at many of the home games—for the next ten years! He was even there the day that the Babe called his famous shot.

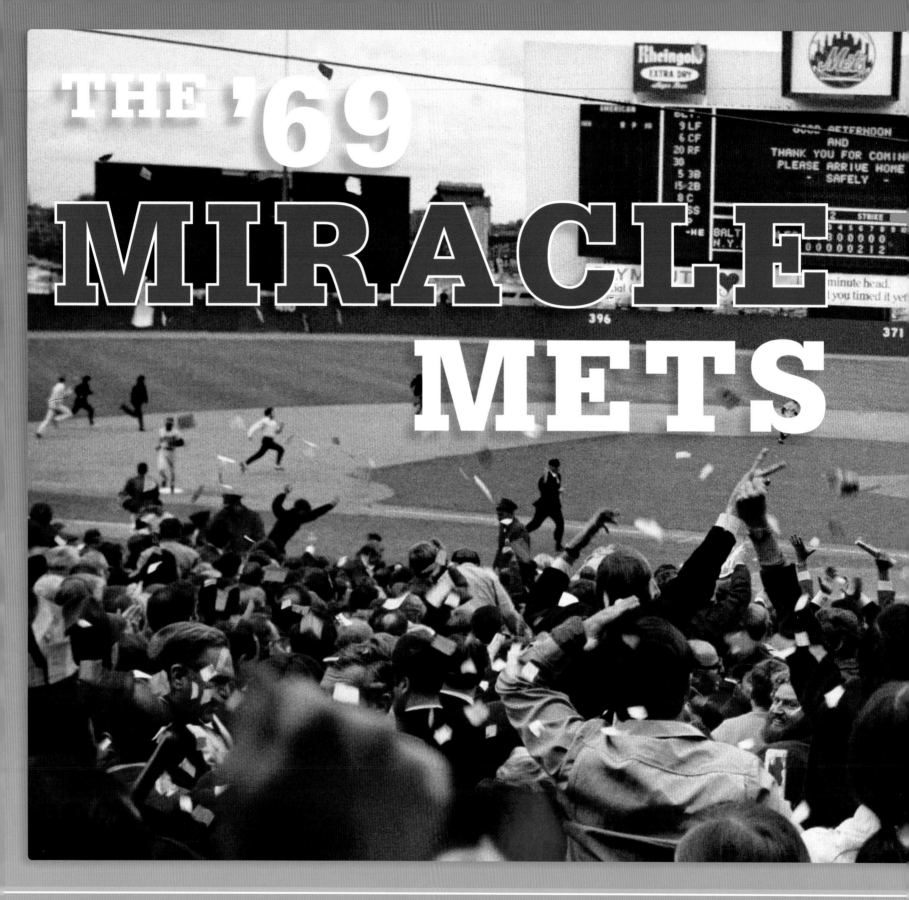

THE '69 MIRACLE METS

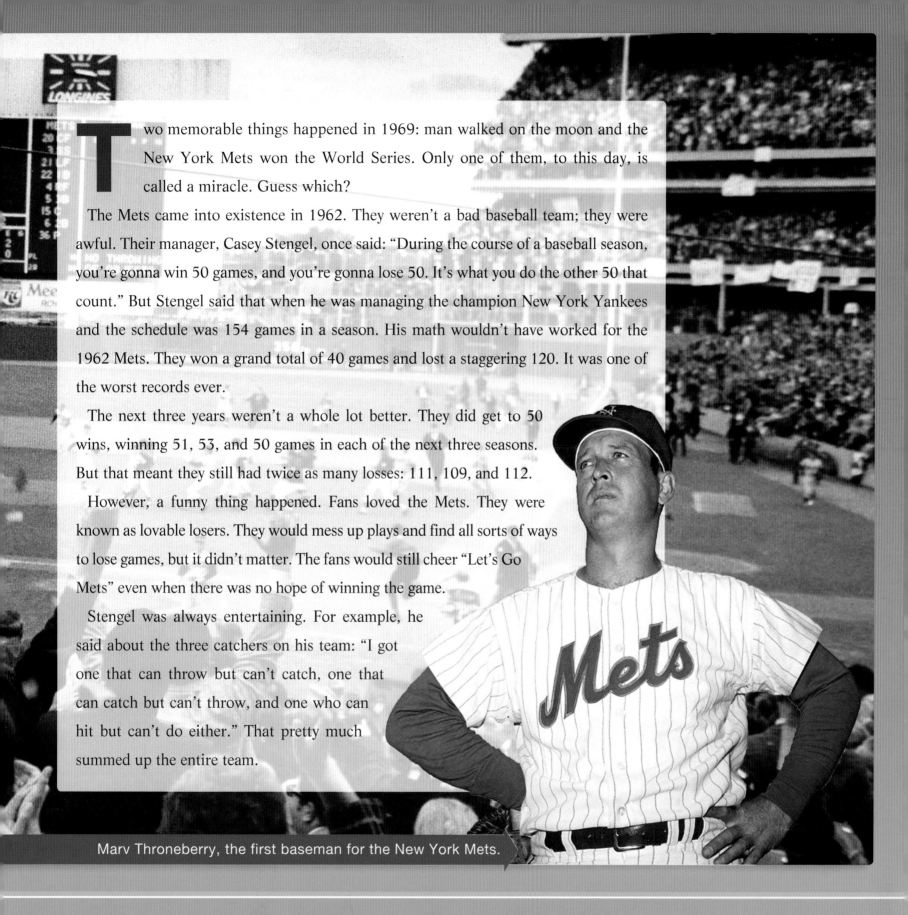

Two memorable things happened in 1969: man walked on the moon and the New York Mets won the World Series. Only one of them, to this day, is called a miracle. Guess which?

The Mets came into existence in 1962. They weren't a bad baseball team; they were awful. Their manager, Casey Stengel, once said: "During the course of a baseball season, you're gonna win 50 games, and you're gonna lose 50. It's what you do the other 50 that count." But Stengel said that when he was managing the champion New York Yankees and the schedule was 154 games in a season. His math wouldn't have worked for the 1962 Mets. They won a grand total of 40 games and lost a staggering 120. It was one of the worst records ever.

The next three years weren't a whole lot better. They did get to 50 wins, winning 51, 53, and 50 games in each of the next three seasons. But that meant they still had twice as many losses: 111, 109, and 112.

However, a funny thing happened. Fans loved the Mets. They were known as lovable losers. They would mess up plays and find all sorts of ways to lose games, but it didn't matter. The fans would still cheer "Let's Go Mets" even when there was no hope of winning the game.

Stengel was always entertaining. For example, he said about the three catchers on his team: "I got one that can throw but can't catch, one that can catch but can't throw, and one who can hit but can't do either." That pretty much summed up the entire team.

Marv Throneberry, the first baseman for the New York Mets.

TOP 10 WORST MLB SEASON RECORDS

YEAR	TEAM	RECORD	PERCENTAGE
1899	Cleveland Spiders	20–134	.130
1916	Philadelphia Athletics	36–117	.235
1935	Boston Braves	38–115	.248
1962	**New York Mets**	**40–120**	**.250**
1904	Washington Senators	38–113	.252
1919	Philadelphia Athletics	36–104	.257
1898	St. Louis Browns	39–111	.260
2003	Detroit Tigers	43–119	.265
1952	Pittsburgh Pirates	42–112	.273
1909	Washington Senators	42–110	.276

cake. His manager supposedly told him, "We would have given you a piece, but we were afraid you'd drop it!"

As the years went by, things didn't improve very much. The Mets finished in last place just about every year for the first seven years of their existence. By 1969, Gil Hodges was their manager, but that season was sure to end the way all the others had for the Mets.

In August, they were nine-and-a-half games behind the first place Chicago Cubs. But

Perhaps the most lovable loser of them all was their first baseman, "Marvelous" Marv Throneberry. The truth is, he wasn't so marvelous. He had a tendency to strike out and make a lot of errors, which was a perfect fit for the Mets.

In one game, he hit a triple, but he was called out for missing second base. When Stengel came out to argue with the umpires, they told Stengel, "Don't bother arguing because he also missed first." The Mets lost the game by one run.

Another time, the team was celebrating Stengel's birthday. Marv complained that he didn't get a piece of birthday

somehow, the Mets started to heat up, and the Cubs started to cool down. And then came a fateful day at Shea Stadium. It was September 9, and the Mets were playing the Cubs. During the game, a black cat walked onto the field and ran around Cubs third baseman Ron Santo while he was standing in the on-deck circle. Was the black cat bad luck for the Cubs? You decide. The Mets beat the Cubs 7–1 that day. In fact, the Mets won their next six games after that to complete a 10-game winning streak. The day after the cat appeared at Shea, the Mets knocked the Cubs out of first place, and Chicago never recovered.

The Mets went on to win 100 games, winning the National League East by eight games over the luckless Cubs. On September 24 at Shea Stadium, the Mets clinched their first title of any kind. In the ninth inning, their future manager, as well as the future manager of the Yankees and Dodgers, Joe Torre, hit into a game-ending double play for St. Louis. It touched off a wild celebration. Fans mobbed the field as the Mets had become the first expansion team to ever win a division title.

Next up for the Mets was the National League Championship Series against the Atlanta Braves and, of course, the Mets were the underdogs. The Braves featured Hank Aaron (the man who beat the Babe), slugger Orlando Cepeda, and pitcher Phil Niekro. But the Mets had a couple of future Hall of Fame pitchers of their own: Tom Seaver and Nolan Ryan. The experts expected pitching to dominate, but it was the hitters who took control. The Mets scored 27 runs in the three games and swept the series. The Mets not only had become the first expansion team to win the pennant, but in just their eighth season of existence, they also became

the quickest pennant winners. The Mets were the 1969 National League champs. Nobody had predicted it. Few could believe it.

And then came the World Series. Again, the experts said the Mets had no chance. They had to play the tough

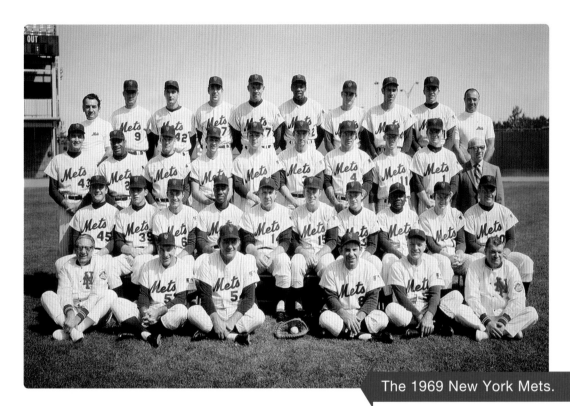

The 1969 New York Mets.

and experienced Baltimore Orioles. Talk about Hall of Famers. The Orioles had outfielder Frank Robinson, third baseman Brooks Robinson, and pitcher Jim Palmer. Baltimore had won 109 games, and they featured four Gold Glove winners for fielding. They had committed the fewest errors in the major leagues. On top of that, they had been to the World Series in 1966 and had swept the Dodgers. There was no way this upstart New York team could beat the powerful Orioles.

And the experts appeared to be correct. The World Series began with a bang. Don Buford of the Orioles led off the bottom of the first with a home run against Seaver. Baltimore was on its way to winning Game 1 of the World Series, 4–1.

The Mets won a tight pitchers duel in Game 2, 2–1. That tied the World Series at one game apiece before shifting to New York. And that's where many of the "miracles" happened.

Game 3 at Shea Stadium began the same way as Game 1 in Baltimore. The home team led off the bottom of the first with a home run. It was hit by center fielder Tommy Agee

Ron Swoboda's game-saving catch.

off Palmer. That was just the beginning of an amazing day for Agee. In the fourth inning, with the Mets leading 3–0, the Orioles had runners on first and third. Elrod Hendricks hit a rocket to left-center field, and Agee running full speed somehow made a twisting backhand catch right at the wall. It saved at least two runs.

LISTEN *to this* **MOMENT TRACK 2**

Agee topped himself in the seventh inning. The Orioles had the bases loaded, and Paul Blair hit a sinking line drive to right-center. Agee dove headfirst onto his stomach to catch the ball, robbing Blair of a hit. Agee probably saved five runs with his two catches as the Mets won Game 3, 5–0, to take a 2–1 Series lead.

There was more to come in Game 4. Another pitchers duel, this time between Seaver and Mike Cuellar. The Mets led 1–0 going into the top of the ninth when right fielder Ron Swoboda became the hero. With runners on first and third, Brooks Robinson hit a sinking line drive. Swoboda swooped in, dove for the ball, and grabbed it backhanded before it hit the ground. Swoboda tumbled on the grass as Frank Robinson tagged up from third and scored the tying run. Even though the Orioles had tied the game, Swoboda had certainly saved the day, forcing the game to go to extra innings. The Mets scored a run in the bottom of the tenth to win 2–1 and take a commanding 3–1 lead in the Series.

THE FIRST SEVEN YEARS IN METS HISTORY

YEAR	MANAGER	RECORD (W–L)	FINISH/ RANK
1962	Casey Stengel	40–120	10
1963	Casey Stengel	51–111	10
1964	Casey Stengel	53–109	10
1965	Casey Stengel and Wes Westrum	50–112	10
1966	Wes Westrum	66–95	9
1967	Wes Westrum and Salty Parker	61–101	10
1968	Gil Hodges	73–89	9
1969	**Gil Hodges**	**100–62**	**1**

Cleon Jones of the Mets.

In Game 5, things got even crazier. The Orioles were leading 3–0 in the sixth when Baltimore pitcher Dave McNally threw a pitch to Cleon Jones. The Orioles claimed the pitch hit the dirt. The Mets claimed the ball hit Jones on his shoe. The ball then bounced into the Mets dugout, and Hodges brought it out to show the umpire. Hodges claimed there was shoe polish on the ball, proving that the ball had indeed hit Jones on his shoe. The umpire agreed and awarded first base to Jones.

That was the beginning of the end for the Orioles. Donn Clendenon followed with a two-run homer, and the Mets were on their way. They won the game 5–3, capturing the World Series four games to one. There was a wild celebration in the clubhouse and later a ticker-tape parade up the "Canyon of Heroes" in Manhattan.

They were the unlikeliest of heroes. A laughingstock team suddenly transformed into World Series champions. There was a joke going around that "Sure, the Mets would win the World Series someday, when man walked on the moon." Both events were considered impossible in the early '60s. But with the help of a black cat, a little shoe polish, and some amazing catches, the Mets actually did it. It was truly a miracle.

HANK BEATS THE BABE

Here now is a little home run history. Before Babe Ruth there was a third baseman for the Philadelphia A's named Frank "Home Run" Baker. He had "Home Run" as his nickname but the most home runs he ever hit in one season was 12. Before Babe Ruth came along, home runs were really not that big of a deal. Then, in 1920, Ruth hit 54 of them. Seven years later, he hit 60. Ruth was now the biggest show in baseball and the reason baseball fans are in love with the home run. No baseball statistic is as revered as the home run. And you can thank Ruth for that.

When Ruth hit his last home run, few people realized that he would never hit another one. The date was May 25, 1935, in Pittsburgh. Ruth was now playing for the Boston Braves. On that day, he hit three home runs in one game: numbers 712, 713, and 714. But at the age of 40, Ruth had hit his last home run. He came down with a cold and retired from baseball a week later. Some experts never thought that record would be broken. Of course, those experts had never heard of somebody named Henry Aaron. That's probably because "Hank" was born in Mobile, Alabama, one year before Babe retired from baseball.

Things were very different in America when Hank was born. African Americans were not allowed to play Major League Baseball. They competed separately in what were called the Negro Leagues. But it wasn't just baseball. African Americans weren't allowed in many hotels or restaurants. In some parts of the country, mainly the south, segregation of the races was a way of life.

Hank grew up poor. He would pick cotton on a farm to earn money. That's where his hands got strong as well as quick. Picking cotton would help Hank to become a

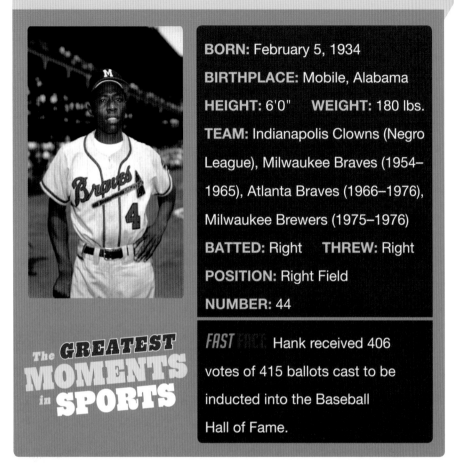

HENRY "HANK" LOUIS AARON

BORN: February 5, 1934

BIRTHPLACE: Mobile, Alabama

HEIGHT: 6'0"   **WEIGHT:** 180 lbs.

TEAM: Indianapolis Clowns (Negro League), Milwaukee Braves (1954–1965), Atlanta Braves (1966–1976), Milwaukee Brewers (1975–1976)

BATTED: Right   **THREW:** Right

POSITION: Right Field

NUMBER: 44

FAST FACT Hank received 406 votes of 415 ballots cast to be inducted into the Baseball Hall of Fame.

The GREATEST MOMENTS in SPORTS

great hitter. Hank's family couldn't afford to buy baseball equipment, so he would practice "baseball" by hitting bottle caps with sticks. In addition, he didn't receive proper coaching. Hank would grip the bat cross-handed. He was a right-handed hitter, but he would put his left hand on top of his right, which is definitely the wrong way to hit. And from these humble beginnings grew one of the greatest players in the history of baseball.

In high school, Hank was not only a great baseball player, but he also excelled at football. In fact, he was so good that he received many scholarship offers to play football, but he turned them all down. He wanted to play baseball. He played for the Mobile Black Bears, a semi-pro team for which he was paid $10 a game. It was there that he caught the attention of a Negro League team called the Indianapolis Clowns. At the age of 18, batting cross-handed, he led the Clowns to the Negro League Championship. After that, the major leagues came calling. Jackie Robinson had broken the color barrier five years earlier. It was now time for Hank to make his mark.

The Clowns sold him to the Boston Braves for $10,000. The Braves then moved to Milwaukee. It was the best $10,000 the Braves ever spent. Hank spent two years in the minor leagues, where his cross-handed hitting style was corrected. He made it to the major leagues at age 20.

Hank wasn't considered a slugger the way Ruth was. Fans came to games to watch Ruth hit homers. But they came to watch Hank perform. And perform he did. He never hit more than 45 home runs in a single season, so there was no reason to expect that he would be the one to challenge the great Ruth for home run supremacy.

But as the years went by, it became obvious that this

Hank Aaron holds the ball from his 715th home run.

had a long winter to get through before he had another crack at the record.

Many baseball fans were excited about Hank's success and couldn't wait for the next season to begin. Unfortunately, there were some bigoted people in America who didn't like the idea that a black man was on the verge of beating out one of the greatest American sports heroes of all time. After the 1973 season ended, things turned ugly. Thousands of people sent him hate mail. He even received death threats. It became a major topic of conversation across the country. Atlanta newspapers received hateful calls from readers who didn't want a black man receiving so much attention. Babe Ruth's widow, Claire Hodgson, came to Hank's defense. She lashed out at the racists, saying Ruth would have been cheering for Hank as he tried to break his record.

Thank goodness Hank survived the off-season without incident and then the 1974 season began. The Braves first three games were in Cincinnati, and the team wanted

kid from Alabama who began in the Negro Leagues had a real chance to match Ruth's record of 714 home runs. While the 1973 baseball season was winding down, the home run chase was on. Hank was closing in on Ruth, but as luck would have it, he fell one short. He had hit 713 home runs, and now Hank and the rest of the country

HANK AARON'S AWARDS

Hank Aaron rounds the bases after hitting his 715th home run.

Selected to play in every All-Star Game from
  1955–1975

1957   National League Most Valuable Player

1958   National League Gold Glove (Right Field)

1959   National League Gold Glove (Right Field)

1960   National League Gold Glove (Right Field)

1982   Inducted into the Baseball Hall of Fame

1999   Named to All-Century Team (Outfield)

Hank to sit out the games so he could attempt to break the record at home in Atlanta. Baseball commissioner Bowie Kuhn objected and ordered Hank to play. His first time at bat, he hit number 714 to tie Ruth! But Hank didn't hit another one in Cincinnati, so the Braves went home to Atlanta to make history.

It was the night of April 8, 1974, and the Braves were playing the Los Angeles Dodgers. A record crowd showed up to watch, and the game was televised nationally by NBC. Hank came to the plate in the second inning and walked. And then in the fourth inning, it happened. Al Downing was pitching, and Hank launched a high fly ball to left field. It was historic. Home run number 715, one more than Ruth. The crowd went wild.

Hank rounded the bases as the all-time home run champion while fireworks exploded overhead. A couple of fans jumped on the field and ran alongside him between second and third base, but they were quickly taken away by security. The celebration continued after he touched home plate. The game was delayed for 10 minutes. His mom and dad were on the field to hug him. They read a telegram from Ruth's widow that said in part, "I know the Babe was rooting for Henry." President Nixon called to offer congratulations. One of the greatest sports records of all time had fallen.

The numbers Hank put up were amazing. By the time he retired, he had set the career record for most runs

LISTEN
to this
MOMENT
TRACK 3

Hank Aaron's teammates congratulate him after breaking the home-run record.

batted in, most career extra-base hits, and most total bases. He had appeared in 24 All-Star Games, and they now give the Hank Aaron Award to the best all-around hitter in each league. Notice, it's not given to the top home run hitter. Yet, despite all his accomplishments, it was the home run chase that captured the imagination of sports fans.

Hank, of course, was later elected to the Hall of Fame, but do you know which mementos he kept with him? Some of the hate letters! They were a reminder of what he had to endure to just play the game of baseball. But

HANK AARON'S CAREER TOTALS

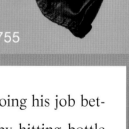

Games: 3,298	Hits: 3,771
At Bats: 12,364	RBIs: 2,297
Runs: 2,174	Home Runs: 755

Hank never got angry. He went about doing his job better than just about anyone. He began by hitting bottle caps with sticks. Along the way, he became an American hero, on and off the field.

THE GREAT ONE

t would take pages to list all of Wayne Gretzky's National Hockey League records. So, just assume that if the record has something to do with scoring, Wayne holds it. Don't even bother to ask who has scored the most goals in a season. The answer is Wayne. In a career? That would also be Wayne. Most assists in a season or a career? Ditto. Most career hat tricks (three or more goals in the same game)? Wayne again. Most goals scored when a teammate was in the penalty box? Same answer. It goes on and on and on.

At last check, Wayne's name was attached to around 60 different scoring records in the National Hockey League record book. There are a couple of other numbers of note, such as four Stanley Cups, nine MVP awards, and the fact that he made the All-Star Game every one of the 20 years he played!

Is there any question why he is simply known as "the Great One"? Actually, if you asked Wayne, he would tell you "the greatest one" is his hockey hero, Gordie Howe. This is the story of the night of October 15, 1989, in Edmonton, Canada. It was the night when the stars were aligned perfectly—when "the Great One" surpassed "the greatest one" to nail down the biggest hockey record of them all.

It all began in the small town of Brantford, Ontario, population around 90,000. The inventor of the telephone, Alexander Graham Bell, once lived there. But so did a

Gordie Howe is Wayne Gretzky's idol and was the holder of the all-time scoring record.

Just one goal for the season. Then again, he was six years old. Everyone else in the league was 10!

Here's something you need to know about Wayne. He wasn't the biggest or the strongest player. He wasn't more than six feet tall or 200 pounds. If you looked at him, you'd think he was rather ordinary. But what wasn't ordinary was his knowledge of the game and his skill. Nobody could match him. They couldn't skate, shoot, or pass as well as this "average-looking" kid from Brantford, Ontario. He went from scoring one goal at the age of six to scoring 378 goals his last year of peewee hockey at the age of 10.

Something else happened when Wayne was 10. He met his boyhood hero. Wayne idolized Gordie Howe, the superstar who played for the Detroit Red Wings. Howe was considered by most experts to be the greatest hockey player in the world. So, it was fitting that Wayne and Howe should meet up at a hockey awards dinner in 1972. What did Howe tell the kid? "Work on your backhand."

By age 16, Wayne had progressed to the Sault Ste. Marie Greyhounds in the Ontario Hockey League. Howe wore number 9, so naturally Wayne wanted to wear that number. But another player had No. 9, so Wayne picked No. 99. That's why he always wore No. 99. And it worked. His first season, he set the all-time Greyhound scoring record with 70 goals and 112 assists for a total of 182 points in just 63 games.

telephone repairman by the name of Walter Gretzky. Walter and his wife Phyllis had five children, the oldest named Wayne.

Wayne loved to skate and play hockey from just about the moment he could stand and lace up skates. His dad got so tired of taking him to the local park to skate that he built a rink in their backyard. That way, Wayne could skate and stickhandle for hour upon hour and never have to leave home. He joined a local hockey league the first chance he got. He didn't exactly set any scoring records.

Wayne Gretzky carries the Stanley Cup with his Edmonton teammates.

WAYNE GRETZKY

BORN: January 26, 1961

BIRTHPLACE: Brantford, Ontario, Canada

HEIGHT: 6'0"   **WEIGHT:** 185 lbs.

TEAM: Edmonton Oilers (1979–1988), L.A. Kings (1988–1996), St. Louis Blues (1996), NY Rangers (1996–1999)

POSITION: Center   **NUMBER:** 99

SHOOTS: Left

The GREATEST MOMENTS in SPORTS

FAST FACT: In 2005, Wayne Gretzky became the head coach of the Phoenix Coyotes.

And so it went for Wayne wherever he played. He made it to the National Hockey League with the Edmonton Oilers in 1979. How did it go? He got an assist in his very first game, but it took him three games to score a goal. By the end of his first season in the league, he scored 51 goals and had 86 assists for a total of 137 points. He was voted the Most Valuable Player in just his first season in the NHL. And then he was the named the MVP for the next seven seasons.

Year after year, Wayne scored at a dizzying pace. In his third year in the NHL, he broke the all-time record for goals in a season by scoring 92. One year, he had a record 163 assists in just 80 games! The numbers kept piling up to heights that nobody had ever seen before. But he had yet to reach one number: 1,850, the number of points scored by his hero, the great Gordie Howe.

August 9, 1988, was a sad day for Edmonton but a happy one for Los Angeles. In the biggest trade in hockey history, Wayne was traded to the Los Angeles

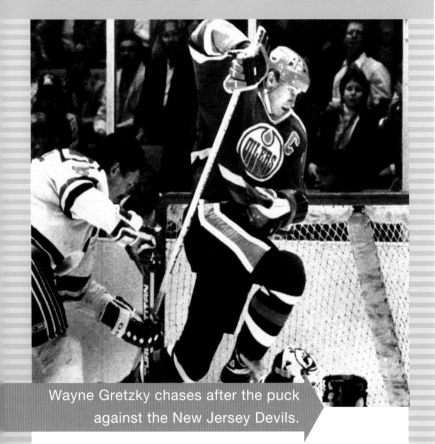

Wayne Gretzky chases after the puck against the New Jersey Devils.

Here are just a few of Wayne Gretzky's records and accomplishments

- 894 goals
- 1,963 assists
- 2,857 total points (goals plus assists)
- 3,239 points (including playoff scoring)
- 20-time All-Star honoree
- Inducted into the NHL Hall of Fame
- His number 99 was retired, not just by the teams he played for but by *every* team in the NHL!

Kings, and that set the stage for his assault to the top of the scoring mountain.

It was the night of October 15, 1989. Wayne was just starting his eleventh season in the NHL and was now a member of the L.A. Kings. As luck would have it, the Kings were playing in Edmonton. A sellout crowd of over 17,000 fans was waiting. Edmonton, of course, was the site of his greatest triumphs, most of all winning four Stanley Cups when he played for the Oilers.

Wayne needed one point to tie Howe's all-time record. And it didn't take long. Early in the game, he recorded an assist. It was career point number 1,850. Howe had reached that total after playing a record 26 years in the NHL. Amazingly, Wayne matched Howe after roughly 10 years. But the crowd wanted more. They wanted to see Wayne break the record.

As the game wore on, it appeared like he wouldn't do it. The Kings were trailing 4–3. They weren't thinking about any records; they were just desperately trying to tie the game. With only a minute to go, the Kings were on the offensive in the Edmonton zone. Wayne set up to the left of the goaltender. The puck suddenly came to him, and in a flash, he had done it. He backhanded the puck into the goal to set the all-time record. Wayne leaped into the air. He was mobbed by his teammates.

LISTEN
to this
MOMENT
TRACK 4

The crowd went wild. One of those on his feet was Howe himself. How fitting. Years earlier, he had told a 10-year-old kid to "work on his backhand." Eighteen years later, that same little kid grew up to backhand a shot that broke Howe's record.

After the goal, play was stopped on the ice for over 10 minutes. Wayne was presented with gifts and then he got on the microphone. He thanked everyone, including his parents and his wife. And then he told the crowd his hero, Gordie Howe, is the "greatest one of all—he is still the greatest."

The ceremony was over, but the game wasn't. It went into overtime tied at four apiece. Now, who do you suppose scored the winning goal for the Kings? I really don't have to tell you, do I? Wayne capped his record-breaking night with the game-winning goal. How perfect. He had told the crowd of his admiration for Howe, but to everyone else, Wayne was "the Great One." And he proved it again that night.

If you went to a hockey game hoping to see Wayne score a goal or an assist, you were rarely disappointed. When all was said and done, on average, he had scored nearly two points, either by a goal or an assist, in every

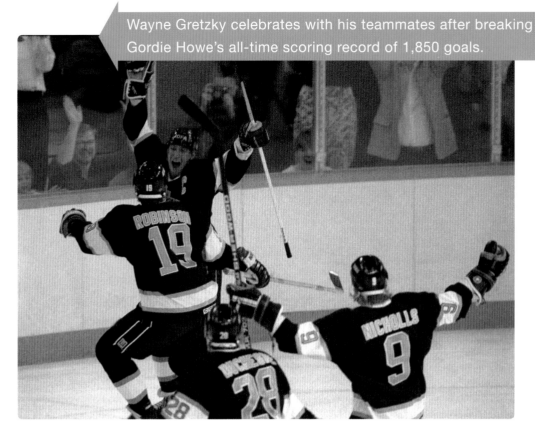

Wayne Gretzky celebrates with his teammates after breaking Gordie Howe's all-time scoring record of 1,850 goals.

A GIFT FOR GRETZKY

One of the gifts Wayne received after breaking Gordie Howe's record was from his former Edmonton teammate MARK MESSIER. It was a diamond bracelet made up of 1.851 carats. The diamonds spelled out the record-breaking number of points: 1851.

game he played. Think about that. He played in 1,487 regular season games and scored 2,857 points. Not bad for a skinny kid who liked to skate around in his backyard in the tiny town of Brantford, Ontario.

A PERFECT 10

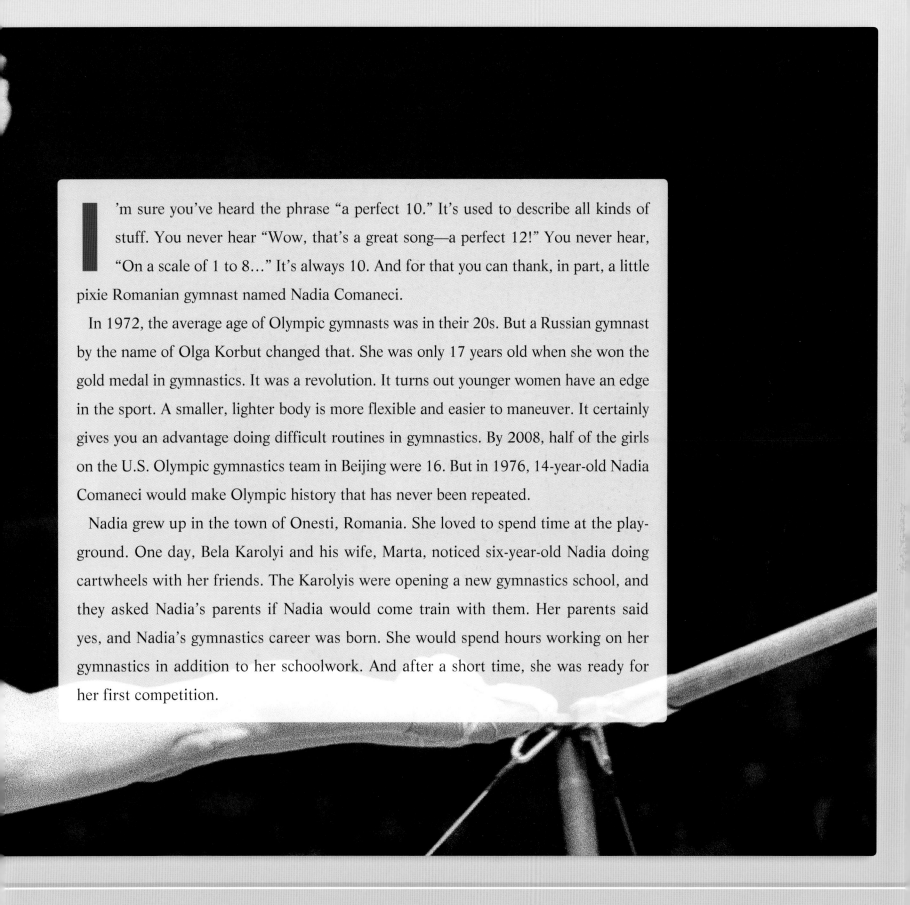

I'm sure you've heard the phrase "a perfect 10." It's used to describe all kinds of stuff. You never hear "Wow, that's a great song—a perfect 12!" You never hear, "On a scale of 1 to 8..." It's always 10. And for that you can thank, in part, a little pixie Romanian gymnast named Nadia Comaneci.

In 1972, the average age of Olympic gymnasts was in their 20s. But a Russian gymnast by the name of Olga Korbut changed that. She was only 17 years old when she won the gold medal in gymnastics. It was a revolution. It turns out younger women have an edge in the sport. A smaller, lighter body is more flexible and easier to maneuver. It certainly gives you an advantage doing difficult routines in gymnastics. By 2008, half of the girls on the U.S. Olympic gymnastics team in Beijing were 16. But in 1976, 14-year-old Nadia Comaneci would make Olympic history that has never been repeated.

Nadia grew up in the town of Onesti, Romania. She loved to spend time at the playground. One day, Bela Karolyi and his wife, Marta, noticed six-year-old Nadia doing cartwheels with her friends. The Karolyis were opening a new gymnastics school, and they asked Nadia's parents if Nadia would come train with them. Her parents said yes, and Nadia's gymnastics career was born. She would spend hours working on her gymnastics in addition to her schoolwork. And after a short time, she was ready for her first competition.

Nadia's graceful performance on the balance beam.

Nadia wasn't an instant success. She finished 13th in the Romanian Junior National Championships. Of course, she was only eight years old! One year later, at the age of nine, she finished first, and she was on her way. She competed in various meets over the next few years, and then came the 1975 European Championships in Norway. Thirteen-year-old Nadia took the championships by storm. She won the gold medal on the beam, the vault, and the uneven bars. She also won the overall gold medal. She won every gold medal at the event except the floor exercise. A star was born!

Next up for Nadia was the 1976 Summer Olympics in Montreal, Canada. Nadia had now "grown up" to the age of 14. But she was not even five feet tall. She checked in at 4 feet 11 inches. And her weight? All of 86 pounds. They say that the "best things come in small packages."

Whoever said that must have been thinking about Nadia.

The Olympic gymnastics competition took place in the Montreal Forum. On the first day of the competition, Nadia performed on the uneven bars. Her routine took just 25 seconds, but it was magical. She effortlessly glided from one bar to the other, twisting and turning with ease. Her dismount was fabulous. She "stuck her landing" exactly as she had planned. She arched her back and stretched out her arms as the crowd cheered with delight. I'm not sure the fans in the Forum really knew what they had just witnessed. To the naked eye, it looked beautiful. To the Olympic judges, it was perfect.

But when the scoreboard flashed her score, it read "1.0." How could she possibly have gotten a one? The top score you could get is a 10. Surely this was worth at least nine points. Then everyone figured it out. Because nobody had ever gotten a 10 before, they didn't build the scoreboard to read out three digits. It couldn't flash a 10.0, so it simply read 1.0. Nadia had just made history. It was the first

NADIA'S OLYMPIC MEDALS

Nadia Comaneci performs her perfect routine on the uneven parallel bars during the 1976 Olympics.

MEDAL	EVENT	OLYMPIC GAMES
Gold	**Balance beam**	**Montreal 1976**
Gold	**Individual all-round**	**Montreal 1976**
Gold	**Uneven bars**	**Montreal 1976**
Gold	Balance beam	Moscow 1980
Gold	Floor exercises	Moscow 1980
Silver	**Team competition**	**Montreal 1976**
Silver	Individual all-round	Moscow 1980
Silver	Team competition	Moscow 1980
Bronze	**Floor exercises**	**Montreal 1976**

Fourteen-year-old Nadia stands in front of a scoreboard during the Olympics.

Today, Nadia Comaneci is the vice chair of the board of directors for the Special Olympics.

perfect 10 from a man or a woman in the history of Olympic gymnastics! She became an instant worldwide celebrity. But there was much more to come.

Nadia was calm while she performed. Didn't smile much. But that didn't matter. Where some gymnasts used their personalities to try to influence the judging, Nadia just let her skills speak for themselves. And they spoke volumes. She followed up that perfect 10 with another. And another! Before the 1976 Olympic gymnastics competition was over, she had scored seven perfect 10s!

Along the way, she collected three gold medals: the all-around, the balance beam, and the uneven bars. It was the greatest performance in the history of women's Olympic gymnastics. All from a 14-year-old weighing 86 pounds. But that wasn't all. Suddenly, young women the world over wanted to participate in gymnastics. She inspired an entire generation of youngsters who wanted to be just like Nadia. And to show you the influence she still has on gymnastics, two of her moves on the uneven bars continue to be named after her: a somersault and a dismount. If you

Another example of Nadia Comaneci's dazzling program during the 1976 Olympic games.

NADIA COMANECI

BORN: November 12, 1961

BIRTHPLACE: Onesti, Romania

HEIGHT (IN 1976): 5'

WEIGHT (IN 1976): 86 lbs.

TEAM: 1976 and 1980 Romanian Olympic gymnastics

SPECIALTIES: Uneven bars, balance beam, floor exercises

FAST FACT: Nadia married American Olympic gymnast and gold medalist Bart Conner.

The *GREATEST* MOMENTS in SPORTS

can't be Nadia on the bars, at least you can try to "do the Nadia."

What Nadia accomplished will never happen again. The scoring system has been changed so that 10 is no longer the highest score a gymnast can receive. It was felt that difficulty and execution should be rewarded. If the routine is exceptionally hard and well-performed, scores can go much higher than 10. For example, in the uneven bars event in Beijing in 2008, the winning score was 16.725. On top of that, the current rule is that a gymnast must be 16 to compete in the Olympics.

So, what Nadia did in Montreal will never be duplicated. She was the first and the youngest to ever score a perfect 10—a score that before her time was impossible to achieve. And because there's a new scoring system and new age rules, it is still impossible for someone to do what she did. Although you'll have to admit "a perfect 10" sounds a whole lot better than "a perfect 16.725," doesn't it?

HITLER'S
OLYMPICS

So, who is the greatest athlete of all time? Just like the argument for greatest moments in sports, picking out the single greatest athlete is open to debate. There are lots of candidates in this book: Babe Ruth, Michael Jordan, and Tiger Woods, just to name a few. Wayne Gretzky is called "the Great One," and Muhammad Ali is simply "the Greatest." But who really is the best? I propose that Jesse Owens has to be in the discussion and so does Jackie Robinson. Tiger may be the greatest golfer of all time, and I think Babe Ruth is the most important baseball player. But "greatest athlete" to me is bigger than just one sport. So, this is my case for Jesse Owens.

Jesse was born James Cleveland Owens in Alabama in 1913. His grandparents were slaves. His parents were poor, so when he was nine years old, they moved to Cleveland, Ohio, in search of better jobs. On his first day of school, the teacher asked him his name. He was known as J. C. for James Cleveland. But because he spoke with a southern drawl, the teacher thought he said "Jesse." It was now his name for life.

Running became his passion. He realized at an early age that he was faster than everyone

Jesse Owens, one of the greatest athletes of all time, in his Ohio State University jersey.

else. So he joined the track team. But he couldn't practice in the afternoons after school with the rest of his team because he had part-time jobs, like delivering groceries and working in shoe-repair shops. So, Jesse would practice in the mornings before school.

Jesse Owens practices his Olympic events in Berlin, Germany.

When he got to high school, he really made a name for himself. At Cleveland East Technical High School, Jesse ran the 100-yard dash in 9.4 seconds, tying the world record. Jesse was just a high school kid and now a star too.

As a result, lots of colleges wanted Jesse to come to their schools and run track. He chose to go to Ohio State University, but it wasn't easy. Oh, the sports stuff was easy for Jesse, but it was what he had to deal with away from the track that was the most difficult: prejudice.

Jesse couldn't live on campus and had to live off-campus with other black athletes. When the team traveled to track meets, he had to stay in "black-only" hotels and eat at "black-only" restaurants. Every once in a while, he was allowed to stay at a "white" hotel. But he couldn't walk in the front door, and he wasn't allowed to use the elevator. On top of all that, he wasn't given a scholarship to attend Ohio State, so he continued to work part-time jobs to pay for his education, all while practicing and going to class.

It was in the spring of 1935, his sophomore year, that Jesse had one of the most amazing days any athlete has ever had. It was on May 25, 1935, during a Big Ten track meet at the University of Michigan in Ann Arbor. Jesse wasn't sure that he could compete because he had fallen down a flight of stairs and hurt his back. But right before the 100-yard dash, he persuaded his coach to let him run. And run he did. Again, Jesse turned in the amazing time of 9.4 seconds, tying his own world record!

Just 15 minutes after that, he competed in the broad jump. Oh, did I forget to mention he was great at jumping too? On his first attempt that day in Ann Arbor, he jumped 26'8.25". He had broken the world record by almost six inches. So, in the span of 15 minutes, he had set one world record and tied another. And he wasn't finished. Next up was the 220-yard dash. He was still in pain. And guess what? He ran the race *and* he set another world record. And he still wasn't done. He then ran the 220-yard low hurdles. And, yup, he set another world record.

In the span of about 45 minutes, Jesse had done something that had never been done before. He set three world records and tied another. Some experts believe that his performance that day in Michigan was the greatest in the history of sports. And would you believe that is not where Jesse made the biggest name for himself? That was still to come.

Next up for Jesse was the 1936 Olympics in Berlin, Germany, commonly known as "Hitler's Olympics." It was the era of Nazi Germany, and Hitler was out to prove to the world that German "Aryan" people were better than everyone else. It was an historic week.

First up was the 100-meter dash. Jesse barely beat out another American by the name of Ralph Metcalfe to win the gold medal. But he was just

JAMES CLEVELAND "JESSE" OWENS

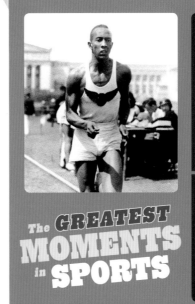

The GREATEST MOMENTS in SPORTS

BORN: September 12, 1913
BIRTHPLACE: Oakville, Alabama
HEIGHT: 5'10" **WEIGHT:** 165 lbs.
SPECIALTIES: Track and Field
NICKNAME: The Buckeye Bullet

FAST FACT: In his junior year at Ohio State, Jesse won every event he ever competed in—all 42 of them.

getting started. The next day was the long jump. During the qualifying session, Jesse surprisingly committed fouls on his first two jumps by stepping over the line. He had one qualifying jump left. Ironically, his German competitor, Luz Long, suggested to Jesse that he start his takeoff several inches behind the jump line to avoid fouling again. That's exactly what Jesse did. On his third and last jump, he qualified for the finals. He then went on to beat his German rival and win his second gold medal. The first to congratulate him and give him a hug was Long. It served to prove that athletes, even from different competing countries, are part of the same "athletic family."

Jesse now had two gold medals, but he wasn't finished. The next day, Jesse ran in the 200-meter dash. He set an Olympic record, beating out Mack Robinson, the older brother of Jackie Robinson. He now had three gold medals, and he still wasn't done.

Four days later, he was picked to run in the 4x100-meter relay. Jesse ran first and got the Americans off to a flying start. By the time they were finished, they had set a world record. Four events, four gold medals for Jesse.

Hitler was furious that his Germans weren't winning more medals, so he refused to congratulate the medal winners. Some people thought that Hitler was intentionally ignoring Jesse, but even Jesse said that Hitler was ignoring *everyone*. The people in the stands definitely weren't ignoring the winners. Jesse was loudly cheered by over 100,000 fans in the stadium, most of them German. They begged him for his autograph.

You would think that when Jesse arrived back home in the United States, he would be a huge hero. And he was. Sort of. They held a ticker-tape parade for him in New York City. But would you believe that when he got to the hotel for the reception, he had to ride up the freight elevator? There was still discrimination, even for a national hero who had just won four gold medals.

In 1976, President Ford awarded Jesse the highest honor a U.S. civilian can receive: the Medal of Freedom.

Jesse waves at the crowds during a ticker-tape parade in New York City after winning four gold medals.

It capped an amazing journey from the grandson of slaves in Alabama, to Ohio State University, to the Olympics, to the White House. From Olympic gold medals to the Medal of Freedom.

But there was one more medal for Jesse. After Jesse's death, President George H. W. Bush awarded him the Congressional Medal of Honor. Not just for winning races, but in recognition of his triumphs for humanity. A fitting final medal for the man I believe to be one of the greatest athletes in the history of sports.

ARTHUR ASHE

To say that Arthur Ashe was a tennis player is like saying Jackie Robinson played baseball or that Barack Obama makes a lot of speeches. Tennis doesn't begin to tell the story. Arthur's story begins in Richmond, Virginia, in 1943. He was basically raised by his father after his mother died when he was just six years old. His dad was a special policeman in charge of Richmond's largest playground for African American kids, right near their house. And it was on the tennis courts of that playground Arthur learned how to play tennis. His father taught him something more important. He told him that you don't get ahead in life by making enemies. You gain by being bright, kind, and helpful to others. They were words that Arthur embraced throughout his incredible lifetime.

Similar to Jesse Owens, Hank Aaron, and Jackie Robinson, Arthur had to deal with segregation. He had to go to "black-only" schools, and he couldn't compete in tennis tournaments on the public courts in Richmond because he was black. So, as a result, he often had to travel great distances to play in tournaments. When he was 15, he became the first African American to ever play in the Maryland Boys Championships. It was the first of many "firsts" for Arthur.

When it came time to go to college, he could have gone to Harvard. Instead, he chose UCLA because of its terrific tennis program. In 1963, he became the first African American named to the U.S. Davis Cup team. He was a team member 10 times, helping the United States win three Davis Cups. And in 1965, he not only won the NCAA tennis tournament in singles (another first for an African American), but he also helped the UCLA Bruins win the NCAA team tennis championship. But maybe more importantly, he became the first youngster on his father's side of the family to graduate from college.

You'd have to admit that a lot of amazing things had happened in his life by the time he graduated from college,

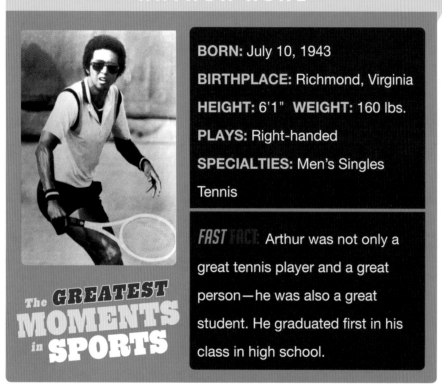

ARTHUR ASHE

BORN: July 10, 1943
BIRTHPLACE: Richmond, Virginia
HEIGHT: 6'1" **WEIGHT:** 160 lbs.
PLAYS: Right-handed
SPECIALTIES: Men's Singles Tennis

FAST FACT: Arthur was not only a great tennis player and a great person—he was also a great student. He graduated first in his class in high school.

The **GREATEST MOMENTS** *in* **SPORTS**

but the best was yet to come. After college, Arthur joined the army. He reached the rank of second lieutenant, and all the while, he continued to play tennis. While still in the army, Arthur competed in the 1968 U.S. Open. He made it to the finals, where he would face a Dutchman named Tom Okker.

In those days, they didn't have a tiebreaker to decide a set. Today, if a set is tied at six games apiece, they play a tiebreaker. The first player to reach seven points (winning by two) wins the set. Back then, when a set was tied 6–6, they kept on playing games. To win a set, a player had to win by two full games. The first set of the 1968 final between Arthur and Okker was a marathon. Arthur eventually prevailed, 14 games to 12!

The entire match also turned into a marathon. Arthur was serving brilliantly that day. He recorded 26 aces (serves that Okker couldn't return). In the end, Arthur was the winner in five long sets. He had become the first black man to win the U.S. Open in tennis. No other black man has won it since.

Arthur made history at every turn. He also won the U.S. National Championship (for amateurs) in 1968, so he was the only man to ever win both the Amateur and Open titles in the same year, a record that will never be broken. And yet, there were still more barriers for Arthur to break down. Two years later, Arthur won the Australian Open, his second Grand Slam win. The Grand Slam of tennis consists of the Australian Open, the French Open, Wimbledon, and the U.S. Open.

By 1975 the top tennis player in the world was Jimmy Connors. Connors was brash and outspoken, the

Jimmy Connors dives to hit a return to Arthur Ashe during the 1975 Wimbledon tournament.

complete opposite of Arthur, who was always the gentleman on and off the court. When Connors met Arthur in the 1975 Wimbledon final, it was called a mismatch. Connors was not only more explosive on the court, but he had played Arthur three previous times and had won them all. Connors was 10 years younger and Arthur, at the age of 33, was clearly on the downside of his career. Everyone predicted that Connors would easily beat Arthur.

It was July 5, 1975, the day of the Wimbledon final. In his previous meetings with Connors, Arthur tried to "hit with him." Connors hit the ball very hard, and Arthur would try to match his strength. But this time, Arthur came up with a new strategy of hitting soft shots. If Connors had a weakness, it was shots hit low to his forehand. So, Arthur would try to dink shots into the front of the court and make Jimmy run up toward the net and reach down for the ball, which he didn't like to do.

And the strategy worked! Arthur easily won the first two sets, 6–1 and 6–1. But Connors roared back, winning the third set, 7–5. And then in the fourth set, Connors raced to a 3–0 lead. It looked for sure like Connors was going to win the fourth, setting up a dramatic and decisive fifth set for the Wimbledon championship.

But Arthur stuck with his plan and then went on a tear. Arthur won six of the next seven games to shock Connors and the tennis world. Arthur won the fourth set 6–4 to win the championship. The first black man to ever play at Wimbledon had become the first black man to win the tournament! And just like the U.S. Open, no black man has won it since. That same year, Arthur became ranked the

Arthur Ashe holds the Wimbledon trophy after defeating Jimmy Connors.

"Success is a journey, not a destination. The doing is often more important than the outcome."

–ARTHUR ASHE

National Junior Tennis League to help kids learn about tennis and positive leadership.

That was the first of dozens of organizations Arthur was involved with. He used his tennis fame to aid others who needed help all over the world. After he stopped playing tennis, he stayed involved with his sport. He became captain of the Davis Cup team. The first two years he was captain, the United States won the Cup. But he stayed even more active in trying to make the world a better place.

Arthur tragically died at the young age of 49. But he accomplished more in those 49 years than just about anyone. These are just a few of his honors: There's a statue of Arthur that stands in his hometown of Richmond, Virginia, the same city where he couldn't compete in tennis because of his race. Arthur was immortalized on a U.S. postage stamp. And, best of all, the arena where the champion of American tennis is crowned every year at the U.S. Open is called Arthur Ashe Stadium.

number one tennis player in the world. Yet another "first" for this groundbreaking kid from Richmond, Virginia.

As great as Arthur was as a player, his list of tennis accomplishments is only part of the story. Remember what his father had said about "helping others"? Arthur spent a lifetime doing just that. In 1969, he cofounded the

In Richmond, Virginia, a statue of Arthur Ashe by Paul DiPasquale emphasizes Arthur's love for educating children.

I've been lucky to have met many of the athletes you are reading about in this book. I have to admit that Arthur was one of my favorites. He was a truly special human being. Sure, he was a great athlete, but he was an even better person. How fitting that every year, the tennis player who does the most to help others is given the Arthur Ashe Humanitarian Award.

ARTHUR ASHE'S GRAND SLAM TITLES

The "Grand Slam" of tennis consists of the Australian Open, the French Open, Wimbledon, and the U.S. Open.

Arthur Ashe and Jimmy Connors shake hands after the final match at Wimbledon in 1975.

YEAR	TOURNAMENT	TITLE
1966	Australian Open	Singles Finalist
1967	Australian Open	Singles Finalist
1968	U.S. Open	Singles Champion
1970	Australian Open	Singles Champion
1970	French Open	Doubles Finalist
1971	Australian Open	Singles Finalist
1971	French Open	Doubles Champion
1971	Wimbledon	Doubles Finalist
1972	U.S. Open	Singles Finalist
1975	Wimbledon	Singles Champion
1977	Australian Open	Doubles Champion

BATTLE
OF THE SEXES

When you discuss the greatest moments in sports, you are talking about some amazing accomplishments. They are groundbreaking, historic, record-setting, or just plain unbelievable. Then, there's the moment that happened on September 20, 1973. It was none of the above. In fact, a case can be made for calling it one of the "Goofiest Sports Moments" in history.

So, why is it in this book? Well, it may not have been the greatest of sports moments in the classic sense of the word, but it was certainly one of the most memorable. And in some ways, it was rather historic. So, here goes. The story of a 55-year-old male blowhard challenging the best female tennis player in the world to a little match—with only the entire world watching.

Bobby Riggs wasn't very tall, and by the 1970s, he certainly wasn't a top tennis player, but he used to be. In the 1940s, Bobby was ranked the top amateur tennis player in the world one year and the top professional player two other years. But he probably made a bigger name for himself as a hustler. He would bet people that he could win at tennis or even golf against players who were better than he was. And then he'd almost always win.

As time went by, some of his hustling became just plain wacky. He would bet somebody he could beat him at tennis by using a frying pan instead of a racket. Or he'd challenge

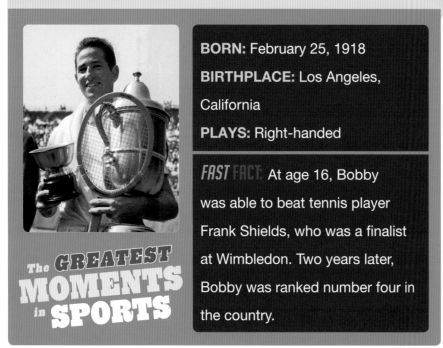

ROBERT "BOBBY" LARIMORE RIGGS

BORN: February 25, 1918

BIRTHPLACE: Los Angeles, California

PLAYS: Right-handed

FAST FACT: At age 16, Bobby was able to beat tennis player Frank Shields, who was a finalist at Wimbledon. Two years later, Bobby was ranked number four in the country.

The GREATEST MOMENTS in SPORTS

BOBBY RIGGS'S GRAND SLAM TITLES

TOURNAMENT	YEAR	SINGLES	DOUBLES	MIXED DOUBLES
Wimbledon	1939	W	W	W
U.S. Open	1939	W	–	–
U.S. Open	1941	W	–	–
U.S. Open	1940	–	–	W

somebody to a golf match and use only one club for the entire round. He may not have been one of the greatest athletes of all time, but he was certainly one of the greatest showmen. And when he boasted to anyone who would listen that at the age of 55 that he could beat any female tennis player alive, he certainly got everyone's attention.

The first player to take Bobby up on his challenge was Margaret Court. Margaret, at the time, was ranked number one in the world. It was just assumed that she would easily win the match and shut up Bobby for good. But it didn't happen that way. On Mother's Day in 1973, Bobby used all of his tricks—lob shots and drop shots—and easily won the match, 6–2, 6–1.

By now, Bobby was in all his glory. He loved taking on the role of the villain and went around telling everyone that men were superior to women, and that women should stay at home and be housewives. This infuriated women all over the world who were struggling to be recognized as the equals of men. Of course, it was mainly an act for Bobby. He knew the bigger a fool he made out of himself, the more interest he would drum up in another tennis match, and the more money he would make. And it all worked. Billie Jean King had seen enough. She now wanted a "piece" of Bobby.

Billie Jean had won three of the four Grand Slam events in 1972. And in 1973, Billie Jean won Wimbledon for the fifth time. But similar to Arthur Ashe, Billie Jean was much more than just a tennis player. She is credited with the explosion of women's sports. Back in the '70s, women were struggling for equality both in and out of sports, and Billie Jean was a leader in that fight. She founded the Women's Tennis Association, which runs the women's pro tour.

And away from tennis, she founded the Women's Sports Foundation, an organization with this stated goal: "To advance the lives of girls and women through sports and physical activity." Billie Jean was a leader in every sense of the word. You can imagine how she felt when this "old man" named Bobby Riggs went around boasting how he could beat all the top female tennis players.

So, the date was set for September 20, 1973, at the Houston Astrodome. Billie Jean was determined to beat Bobby for lots of reasons. She said: "I thought it would set us back 50 years if I didn't win that match. It would ruin the women's tour and affect all women's self-esteem." This was no ordinary tennis match. By the time they met, it had truly become "the battle of the sexes." It seemed as if all of womanhood was on trial that night on the tennis court.

Billie Jean King and Bobby Riggs face off during a press conference.

Billie Jean King played softball when she was younger before she played tennis.

Billie Jean King arrives on a throne before her match with Bobby Riggs.

BILLIE JEAN KING'S
GRAND SLAM TITLES

TOURNAMENT	YEAR	SINGLES	DOUBLES	MIXED DOUBLES
Wimbledon	1961	-	W	-
Wimbledon	1962	-	W	-
Wimbledon	1965	-	W	-
Wimbledon	1966	W	-	-
Wimbledon	1967	W	W	W
Wimbledon	1968	W	W	-
Wimbledon	1970	-	W	-
Wimbledon	1971	-	W	W
Wimbledon	1972	W	W	-
Wimbledon	1973	W	W	W
Wimbledon	1974	-	-	W
Wimbledon	1975	W	-	-
Wimbledon	1979	-	W	-
Australian Open	1968	W	-	W
French Open	1967	-	-	W
French Open	1970	-	-	W
French Open	1972	W	W	-
U.S. Open	1964	-	W	-
U.S. Open	1967	W	W	W
U.S. Open	1971	W	-	W
U.S. Open	1972	W	-	-
U.S. Open	1973	-	-	W
U.S. Open	1974	W	W	-
U.S. Open	1976	-	-	W
U.S. Open	1978	-	W	-
U.S. Open	1980	-	W	-

Billie Jean and Bobby play hard inside the Houston Astrodome in Texas.

And what a night it was! Billie Jean first entered the arena as if she were Cleopatra. She was held aloft on her throne by four muscular men. Next came Bobby. He was wheeled out in a rickshaw pulled by beautiful models. This was definitely not your average tennis match. And it wasn't your normal audience either. Over 30,000 fans packed into the Astrodome to watch in person that night. It was the biggest live crowd ever for tennis. And it was estimated that 50 million more were watching on television. It would be the most-watched tennis match in history.

Unlike Margaret Court, Billie Jean was ready for all of Bobby's tricks. Those dink shots and lob shots weren't going to work. Billie Jean stayed deep in the court, and she ran her older opponent from side to side. Billie Jean won the first set 6–4 and didn't stop there. She won the second set 6–3 and also the third by the same 6–3 score. It was a complete and dominant victory. But it wasn't just the fact that she won a tennis match. Billie Jean proved that men (despite what Bobby kept claiming) were not superior to women. Women could be athletes just like men.

Billie Jean may have won the "Battle of the Sexes," but she advanced the idea of "Equality of the Sexes" even more. No, this wasn't just another tennis match. And while it may not have been truly one of the greatest moments in sports history, it turned out to be one of the most significant. A woman had beaten a loudmouthed hustler at his own game. And along the way, she struck a blow for women the world over.

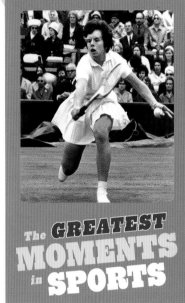

BILLIE JEAN KING

BORN: November 22, 1943

BIRTHPLACE: Long Beach, California

HEIGHT: 5'4.5"   **WEIGHT:** 134 lbs.

PLAYS: Right-handed

FAST FACT Billie Jean was the first female athlete in any professional sport to win $100,000 in prize money in a single season!

The **GREATEST MOMENTS in SPORTS**

Tennis rackets used in the "Battle of the Sexes" tournament were made of wood and had long handles and very small areas of string to hit the ball with. "Oversized head" rackets were constructed in the mid-1970s to create larger "sweet spots" for hitting the ball. Over the years, tennis rackets have been made from steel, aluminum, fiberglass, titanium, and carbon in order to make them lighter and faster.

THE GREATEST GAME EVER PLAYED

So, out of the millions of games played in every sport, can you refer to one game as the greatest? Well, there is one game that was played that claims that title. It was a football game played at Yankee Stadium on December 28, 1958. And it matched up the Baltimore Colts against the New York Giants. Before 1967, there was no Super Bowl. To crown the champions of the National Football League, they played a 60-minute championship game. Only, in 1958, the game lasted longer than 60 minutes. That had never happened before. And it's just one of the reasons why to this day, the 1958 NFL Championship Game is still referred to as "the Greatest Game Ever Played."

Now, if you're going to call a game "the greatest," you would think that it was played perfectly with amazing plays. But the 1958 Championship Game was far from perfect. Six times in the game, a team fumbled the ball away. There were missed field goals and interceptions too. This was not exactly a perfect game. But what made this game "the greatest" was how it wound up and the impact it had on American sports.

The 1958 New York Giants were a glamorous team. Their players were household names. They had a cover-boy running back in Frank Gifford and a bruising linebacker named Sam Huff. And what a coaching staff! Their offensive coordinator was Vince Lombardi, who later guided the Green Bay Packers to win both Super Bowl I and Super Bowl II. If Lombardi's name sounds familiar to you, maybe it's because they give football teams the Vince Lombardi Trophy when they win the Super Bowl! New York's defensive coordinator was Tom Landry. Later, as coach of the Dallas Cowboys, he too went on to win two Super Bowls. In all, six Giants players plus Lombardi

The Giants running back Frank Gifford.

and Landry eventually made it to the Pro Football Hall of Fame. And with that collection of talent, they arrived at the 1958 NFL Championship Game.

The 1958 Baltimore Colts also had six players who would make the Hall of Fame, led by one of the greatest

> The 1958 Championship Game was one of the first pro football games ever televised nationally. But if you lived in New York, you couldn't watch it. In those days, home games were not televised. So, even though football fans were watching the game all across America, fans in New York couldn't watch their own team!

quarterbacks of all time, Johnny Unitas, and defensive linemen Art Donovan and Gino Marchetti. Their coach, Weeb Ewbank, was also a future Hall of Famer.

The 1958 Championship Game was played in late December, unlike the Super Bowl, which is now played in early February. The season was shorter back then, and there weren't any scheduled playoff games. So, on December 28, the Colts met the Giants to determine which team was the best in professional football. And for the first time, the championship game was televised nationally.

Midway through the game, there was no reason to believe that this game would someday be called "the greatest." Baltimore led 14–3, with both of their touchdowns set up by fumbles by Gifford. The game turned around early in the third quarter. The Colts were knocking on the door, ready to score another touchdown, but the Giants defense stiffened. Baltimore turned the ball over on downs. The Giants then proceeded to march 95 yards for a touchdown. And then, early in the fourth quarter, Giants quarterback Charlie Conerly threw a 15-yard touchdown pass to Gifford. The Giants had taken the lead 17–14.

It was now nearing the end of the game, and lots of crazy things were happening. For one, somebody accidentally disconnected the TV cable and the game was knocked off television for several minutes. They corrected the mistake, but it was very nearly "the Greatest Game That Nobody Ever Saw!" In addition, Marchetti broke his leg making a key play late in the game. It was the first time his parents were able to watch him play on television, but he had to watch the dramatic ending from the sidelines.

And what an ending it was. Baltimore trailed by three points with two minutes to go. They were on their own 14-yard line. It was then that Unitas engineered one of the greatest drives in football history. He marched his team down the field thanks to his favorite wide receiver, Raymond Berry. He kept throwing passes to Berry—and Berry kept catching them. The Colts made it all the way down to the Giants 13-yard line with just seven seconds to play. Steve Myhra then came onto the field to attempt a 20-yard field goal. The kick was good, and the score was tied at 17.

Time had run out. So, now what? In those days, they didn't play overtimes. When an NFL game ended in a tie, that was the final score. But this was a championship game. You have to have one champion, not cochampions. Even the players didn't know what would happen next. And then the officials announced they would flip a coin to decide who gets the ball. Then, they would play overtime to decide the title. The first team that scores wins. Would you believe some of the players had never heard of overtime before? So, there you had it—the first ever nationally televised NFL championship game. And as an added bonus, the Giants and Colts were going to play the first sudden-death overtime in NFL history.

The Giants won the toss and elected to receive. But their offense went nowhere, and after three plays, they were forced to punt. The Colts took over on their own 20 and went on a 13-play 80-yard drive. It was capped off by fullback Alan Ameche charging into the end zone from the one-yard line. The Baltimore Colts were NFL champs, beating the Giants 23–17.

Was it "the Greatest Game Ever Played?" Thanks to the overtime and the television coverage, that one game is credited for pro football exploding as a national passion. Today, pro football is considered by many to be the most popular sport in America. The highest-rated TV show of

Baltimore's Lenny Moore (No. 24) takes a handoff from quarterback Johnny Unitas.

any kind every year is the Super Bowl. And the rise in popularity all began with that December football game in 1958. It may not have been truly the greatest football game ever played, but it was clearly the most significant.

THE GREATEST PLAY IN SUPER BOWL HISTORY

So, if a career or a game can be called the greatest, can a single play? It's probably impossible to pick out one single play from the millions in sports history. So, let's narrow it down a little. How about the greatest play in Super Bowl history? Bingo. And it wasn't made by superstars like Joe Montana or Joe Namath; it was made by a player who hardly anyone had ever heard of. But after he made one catch, everyone knew his name. His name is David Tyree, and he was a wide receiver for the New York Giants in Super Bowl XLII. How unlikely was it that David would make a big catch? Well, he hadn't started a single game for the entire season, and he was hardly used as a wide receiver. All season long, he had made just four catches for a total of 35 yards. That's it. And when it came to Super Bowl XLII in 2008, David wasn't even sure he would be used to catch passes.

David played high school football in Montclair, New Jersey. He was a terrific football player and landed a scholarship to play college football at Syracuse University. In addition to being an excellent wide receiver, he was even better on special teams coverage. Special teams are involved in kicks and punts. During his time at Syracuse, he blocked six punts. The pros took notice.

When it came time for the NFL draft, David was drafted in the sixth round by the New York Giants. That's not real high, but his ability on special teams helped him make the roster. During his first year, he was named the top special teams rookie in the NFL.

David continued to be valuable on special teams. During a game in 2005, he blocked a punt and was eventually named to the Pro Bowl. He was now considered one of the best players in the league. But not for his pass-catching.

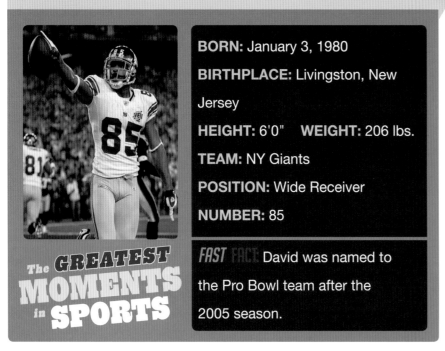

DAVID TYREE

BORN: January 3, 1980

BIRTHPLACE: Livingston, New Jersey

HEIGHT: 6'0"   **WEIGHT:** 206 lbs.

TEAM: NY Giants

POSITION: Wide Receiver

NUMBER: 85

FAST FACT David was named to the Pro Bowl team after the 2005 season.

The GREATEST MOMENTS in SPORTS

By the time the 2007 season was winding down, his playing pattern remained the same. He had started only five games in his career, and he had caught 54 passes. But he had been in the league for five years, so 54 catches amounted to fewer than one a game. He was anything but a big-time wide receiver. If you asked football fans who would be likely to make the most amazing, unbelievable catch in Super Bowl history, nobody would name David. In fact, most football fans around the country really didn't know who he was.

When the 2007 season ended, the Giants began an improbable run to the Super Bowl. Because they qualified for the playoffs as a wild-card team, they wouldn't play any of their games at home. It didn't matter. First, they beat Tampa Bay and then Dallas. And when they beat Green Bay in overtime in freezing conditions, they had made it all the way to Super Bowl XLII in Glendale, Arizona. During that play-off run, David made exactly one catch in Green Bay. The play went for four yards.

The Giants Super Bowl opponent was the heavily favored New England Patriots. They had not lost a game the entire season. Going into the Super Bowl, they were 18–0. No NFL team had ever been 19–0 in a single season. The Patriots were quarterbacked by the great Tom Brady. He and the Patriots had already won three Super Bowls, and he was the Super Bowl MVP twice. By comparison, Eli Manning was the Giants quarterback, and his claim to fame was that his more-famous brother Peyton Manning of the Indianapolis Colts had won Super Bowl MVP award the year before.

Super Bowl XLII turned out to be an exciting game. Early in the fourth quarter, Manning threw a 5-yard touchdown pass to David, and the Giants took the lead. It was his first touchdown of the entire season! But the Patriots would not be denied. They later drove down the field, and with just 2:42 left in the game, Brady hit Randy Moss for a 6-yard touchdown. The favored

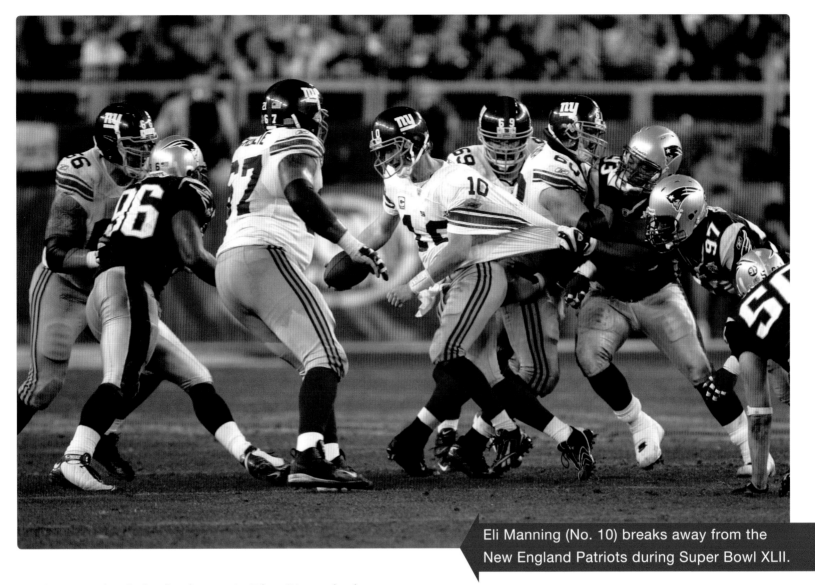

Eli Manning (No. 10) breaks away from the New England Patriots during Super Bowl XLII.

Patriots regained the lead 14–10. The Giants had one last chance, and that's when it happened.

Manning started to drive the Giants downfield. They reached their own 44-yard line and faced a critical third down and five yards to go with just 1:15 left in the game. Manning dropped back to pass, but the Patriots defenders came charging after him. Linebacker Adalius Thomas grabbed a handful of Manning's jersey,

There is another play in history known as "the Catch." In the 1982 NFC Championship Game, JOE MONTANA threw a winning touchdown pass to DWIGHT CLARK. The San Francisco 49ers beat the Dallas Cowboys that day. That play was always called "the Catch."

THE HISTORY OF THE HELMET

David Tyree's helmet helped his team win the Super Bowl, but, of course, helmets are meant to protect the players' heads!

- Although helmets were not mandatory until the 1930s, the first leather football helmet was created and worn in 1893. Early helmets looked like aviator caps and did not have much protection.

- In the 1930s and 1940s, helmets gained more padding, and the leather exterior got tougher.

- Every team's helmet looked similar—they did not have any team logos. But in 1948, someone painted ram horns on a leather helmet, and the Los Angeles Rams became the first team to popularize logos on their professional helmets.

- In 1949, plastic helmets were accepted for use in the NFL.

- It wasn't until the 1970s and 1980s when teams really started to decorate their helmets.

Helmets continually improve as the years go on to better protect the players!

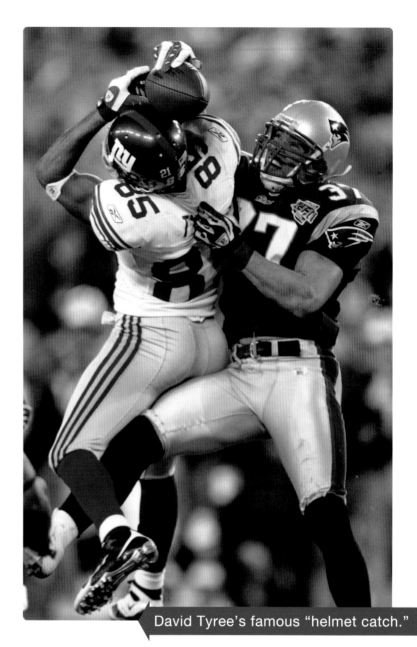

David Tyree's famous "helmet catch."

but Manning somehow got away and just flung the ball far downfield.

And that's when the football found a most unlikely hero. David leaped into the air, with defensive back Rodney Harrison draped all over him. First, David

Eli Manning (No. 10) and David Tyree (No. 85) celebrate their Super Bowl win over the Patriots.

ELI MANNING

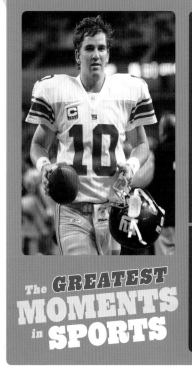

The GREATEST MOMENTS in SPORTS

BORN: January 3, 1981

BIRTHPLACE: New Orleans, Louisiana

HEIGHT: 6'4"   **WEIGHT:** 225 lbs.

TEAM: NY Giants

POSITION: Quarterback

NUMBER: 10

FAST FACT: Eli won the 2008 Super Bowl MVP, which was the year after his brother Peyton won it for the Indianapolis Colts.

grabbed the ball with two hands, but then his left hand fell away from the ball. With his right hand, he pinned the ball against his helmet while he was simultaneously falling backward on top of Harrison. He somehow held on to the ball for an absolutely amazing 32-yard play down to the Patriots 24-yard line.

LISTEN *to this* **MOMENT TRACK 5**

Four plays later, Manning found Plaxico Burress in the end zone for the game-winning touchdown. The Giants had pulled off an incredible upset, beating the Patriots 17–14. And it was all set up by the most amazing catch in Super Bowl history. David was now an instant hero. Everyone wanted to meet him. He appeared on TV shows around the country. Newspapers and TV stations held contests to find a name for his amazing catch. My favorite was "Heads Up." But in the end, people just referred to it as "the Catch." And it was made by one of the most unlikely heroes in football history.

THE STANFORD BAND PLAY

The play covered 55 yards. The most famous football player in the stadium wasn't involved, but a trombone player in the band was. Sound interesting? It's become known as the "Stanford Band Play," and Stanford wasn't even the team with the ball. And while you can make an argument that this wasn't the greatest play, you can make an argument that it was the craziest. And when it comes to the Greatest Moments in Sports, that's good enough for me.

The date was November 20, 1982, at California Memorial Stadium in Berkeley. The California Golden Bears were hosting their rivals, the Stanford Cardinal. Stanford came into the game with a 5–5 record, and they needed a win to be invited to a bowl game. In addition, their great quarterback John Elway was playing his last game.

Stanford was trailing California 19–17. And with time running out, Elway led the Cardinal on a drive down the field. They reached the 18-yard line with just seconds remaining, so Elway called a time-out. The next play was a 35-yard field goal by Mark Harmon. Stanford had taken a 20–19 lead. But Elway had called the time-out too quickly. If he would have waited a couple of seconds to call the time-out, Harmon's field goal would have been the last play of the game, ensuring a Cardinal victory.

There were still four seconds left on the clock, but the Cardinal players spilled onto the field to celebrate. Stanford was penalized for its early celebration. So, when Stanford kicked off, instead of kicking from its 40-yard line, the Cardinal players were backed up to their own 25. Would those 15 yards make a difference? There were only four seconds left. What could possibly happen? The Stanford players and all their fans figured the game was over. But it wasn't.

With four seconds left, there was time for one final kickoff. And Harmon squib-kicked it—a short kick. California wasn't exactly organized. They had only 10 men on the field instead of the normal 11. That wasn't a penalty, but it was one more disadvantage that was facing the Bears in those final four seconds. And as Joe Starkey, announcing the game on the radio, told his audience, "Only a miracle can save the Bears now!"

And that's exactly what happened. Kevin Moen fielded the ball for Cal and had nowhere to go, so he lateraled the ball to Richard Rodgers, who was standing to his

California's Kevin Moen (No. 26) and Keith Kartz (No. 79) after Moen scored the winning touchdown against Stanford.

left. Rodgers tried to run, but he was quickly surrounded by Stanford players. Because he couldn't go anywhere, he threw the ball behind him to Dwight Garner. At this point, three Cal players had touched the ball, but they had made no forward progress.

Here's where things got interesting. Garner ran about five yards and was greeted by a host of Stanford players. Just as he was being tackled, he pitched the ball back to Rodgers. But lots of people thought that Garner had been tackled before he got rid of the ball. Stanford players started to celebrate (again) that they had won the game. And the entire Stanford Cardinal marching band, which numbered 144 strong, started coming onto the field. They were waiting behind the end zone for the game to end, and when they thought Garner was tackled, they started marching through the end zone and into the field of play.

But the game wasn't over! Rodgers started to make a little progress and had reached the Stanford 45-yard line. So, by now, the ball had been handled four times by Cal, and they had gained 10 yards. Rodgers was about to get caught, so he flipped the ball to Mariet Ford, and Ford made some real progress. But as he was running toward the end zone, the Stanford band was marching up the field. Ford kept running, and near the 25-yard line, he was about to be tackled by three Stanford players, so he just blindly threw the ball over his shoulder. It was caught by Moen, the first player to touch the ball during this play, five laterals and 30 yards ago.

By now, the field was a complete mess—players, band members, officials everywhere. Some players thought the game was over; others had no idea what was going on. Band members started scattering when they saw what was happening, and Moen kept running. He made it all the way into the end zone. Standing in the end zone was trombone player Gary Tyrrell. Moen flattened him—ran right over him. And now, the play was over.

But did it count? Were all those laterals legal? (A lateral can't go forward; it has to go sideways or backward.) Had Garner really been tackled way up field? The officials huddled and quickly signaled that it was indeed a touchdown! Starkey started screaming on the radio, "The Bears have won, the Bears have won! Oh my God, the most amazing, sensational, traumatic, heartrending…exciting, thrilling finish in the history of college football!"

LISTEN
to this
MOMENT
TRACK 6

The "miracle" had happened. Cal had won the game, 25–20.

It didn't occur in a bowl game. It didn't decide a championship. "The Stanford Band Play," or just "the Play," as it came to be called, just happened one Saturday afternoon in Berkeley, California, in 1982. They had never seen anything like it in the entire history of college football.

And if you ever go to the College Football Hall of Fame in South Bend, Indiana, you'll see some amazing artifacts. You can see the helmet worn by the great running back Jim Brown at Syracuse University in 1956. You can find a sweatshirt worn by the legendary Notre Dame football coach Knute Rockne. And you can also see something else that you don't expect to find in a Football Hall of Fame. If you walk into the Great Rivalries exhibit, you can find the trombone and trombone case that belonged to Gary Tyrrell.

THE YOUNGEST MASTER

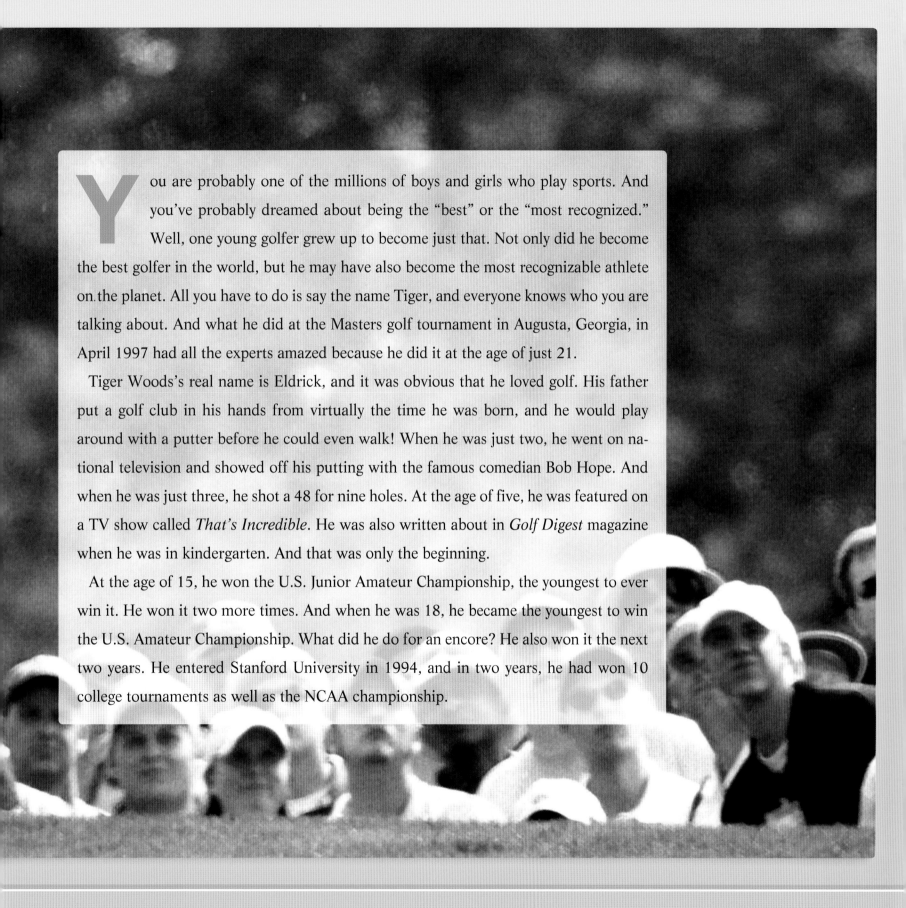

You are probably one of the millions of boys and girls who play sports. And you've probably dreamed about being the "best" or the "most recognized." Well, one young golfer grew up to become just that. Not only did he become the best golfer in the world, but he may have also become the most recognizable athlete on the planet. All you have to do is say the name Tiger, and everyone knows who you are talking about. And what he did at the Masters golf tournament in Augusta, Georgia, in April 1997 had all the experts amazed because he did it at the age of just 21.

Tiger Woods's real name is Eldrick, and it was obvious that he loved golf. His father put a golf club in his hands from virtually the time he was born, and he would play around with a putter before he could even walk! When he was just two, he went on national television and showed off his putting with the famous comedian Bob Hope. And when he was just three, he shot a 48 for nine holes. At the age of five, he was featured on a TV show called *That's Incredible*. He was also written about in *Golf Digest* magazine when he was in kindergarten. And that was only the beginning.

At the age of 15, he won the U.S. Junior Amateur Championship, the youngest to ever win it. He won it two more times. And when he was 18, he became the youngest to win the U.S. Amateur Championship. What did he do for an encore? He also won it the next two years. He entered Stanford University in 1994, and in two years, he had won 10 college tournaments as well as the NCAA championship.

AMATEUR WINS

1991 U.S. Junior Amateur Championship

1992 U.S. Junior Amateur Championship

1993 U.S. Junior Amateur Championship

1994 U.S. Amateur Championship

1994 Western Amateur

1994 Pacific Northwest Amateur

1995 U.S. Amateur Championship

1996 U.S. Amateur Championship

1996 NCAA Championship

1996 NCAA West Regional

1996 Pac-10 Championship

MAJOR CHAMPIONSHIP WINS

1997 The Masters

1999 PGA Championship

2000 U.S. Open

2000 British Open

2000 PGA Championship

2001 The Masters

2002 The Masters

2002 U.S. Open

2005 The Masters

2005 British Open

2006 British Open

2006 PGA Championship

2007 PGA Championship

2008 U.S. Open

Tiger Woods thinks about his next move during the 1996 U.S. Amateur Golf Championship.

The week after he won his third consecutive U.S. Amateur title, Tiger turned pro. He had played in some professional tournaments as an amateur. In fact, he tied the record at the British Open for the best score ever by an amateur when he was 19. So, in 1996, he joined the Professional Golfers' Association (PGA) Tour at the age of 20. In order to qualify for the pro tour in 1997, he had to finish among the top 125 money winners for the entire year. But Tiger joined late in the golf season, and there were just seven tournaments left to play.

What happened next was one of his greatest accomplishments. Tiger won two of those seven tournaments and finished in the top 5, five weeks in a row against the greatest golfers in the world! He won nearly $800,000 and easily qualified for the PGA Tour in 1997. He had done some unbelievable things, all by the age of 20. And he was about to top them all.

The sports world couldn't wait to see how 21-year-old Tiger would do at the first major golf tournament of 1997, the Masters. The first round was on Thursday, April 10. A big crowd had gathered to watch this golfing sensation, but to everyone's surprise, Tiger flopped. His drives off the tee went everywhere except on the fairway. He would drive the ball into the woods, and the fans lining the fairways had to scatter.

As the first nine holes went on, the fans lost interest. They started to disperse to find other golfers to watch instead. Tiger finished the first nine holes with a 40. The big star had gone bust. Tiger later admitted that he was "horrible," and he was pretty mad at himself.

ELDRICK "TIGER" WOODS

BORN: December 30, 1975
BIRTHPLACE: Cypress, California
HEIGHT: 6'1" **WEIGHT:** 185 lbs.
PLAYS: Right-handed
COLLEGE: Stanford University
BEGAN PROFESSIONAL CAREER: 1996

The **GREATEST MOMENTS** *in* **SPORTS**

FAST FACT: Tiger was only nine months old when he first swung a golf club.

Tiger Woods has an average clubhead speed of 125 miles per hour.

Nobody had ever shot a 40 for nine holes and still won the Masters. Then again, nobody had ever seen the likes of Tiger Woods before.

So, how did he respond on the back nine? He birdied three of the first four holes. And then, on the 15th hole, he had a 3 on the 500-yard par 5. An eagle! Tiger finished the back nine with an amazing 30, just one

Tiger got his first hole-in-one on May 12, 1982. He was only 6 years old!

"The only thing I want is a green jacket in my closet. Whatever I have to do to win is fine."

—TIGER WOODS DURING THE 1997 MASTERS TOURNAMENT

off the record at the Augusta National Golf Club, where the Masters is played every year. Tiger had shot a 70 for the first round. With the eyes of the golf world upon him, he had turned disaster into brilliance. He was just three shots off the lead after one round of the 1997 Masters.

Round two was nothing like round one. It was brilliant from beginning to end. Tiger was driving the ball farther than anyone. He was hitting pinpoint iron shots to the greens. And his putting was flawless. He shot an amazing 66. When the sun went down on Friday, April 11, the 21-year-old sensation was leading the Masters by three shots. He had become the youngest to ever lead the prestigious Masters at the halfway mark.

How could Tiger do any better than a 66 during Saturday's third round? By shooting a 65! His drives continued to explode off the tee, and his amazing lead continued to grow. By the end of play on Saturday, he was not only the leader by nine shots, but he had tied the record for the lowest 54-hole total in Masters history: 201. His 9-shot lead broke the all-time record.

The experts said Tiger "just had to show up" on Sunday to win the tournament. But Tiger wasn't about to stop playing his best. On Sunday, he shot a 69. That gave him a grand total of 270 for all four rounds. It was the lowest score anybody had ever shot in the history of the Masters. And he had won the 1997 Masters by an incredible 12 shots! It was not only the largest margin of victory in the history of the Masters but the largest of all the major golf tournaments ever played, which dated all the way back to the British Open in 1860.

It was simply one of the most unbelievable performances in the history of golf. Not only had he become the youngest Masters champion at the age of 21. Not only did he have the lowest score ever and the biggest margin of victory, but he had become the first black man to win a major golf tournament. Tiger said maybe kids who never thought about playing golf would pick up clubs. And maybe that's what he is proudest of.

Tiger Woods wears the famous green jacket and holds a replica of the Masters Trophy after winning the tournament.

The **GREEN JACKET** is awarded to the winner of the Masters tournament every year, and it just may be the most famous piece of golf clothing in the world.

CLAY DEFEATS LISTON

Tiger Woods may be the most recognized athlete on the planet, but he's got some competition. It comes from a boxing champion born in Louisville, Kentucky, in 1941 named Cassius Clay. You may not know that name, but you've probably heard of Muhammad Ali. They are one and the same. And you can argue that in his prime, he was not only the best boxer around, but he was the biggest personality in all of sports.

His early career as an amateur was amazing. The Golden Gloves competition is open to amateur boxers all over the country. Young Cassius won the Kentucky Golden Gloves title six different times. He then went on to capture two straight national Golden Gloves championships.

It was only natural that this tremendous young fighter would try out for the Olympics. In Rome, Italy, at the age of 18, he won the light heavyweight gold medal. More interesting than the fact that he won is how he won. He was a showman. He would dance around the ring with catlike quickness. He was difficult for opponents to hit. He was fast and powerful.

But he was also loud and cocky. He would brag that he was going to win and then he'd go out and do it. In the final at the Olympics, he showed the world something they hadn't seen. He demolished his Polish opponent while dancing around the ring taunting him.

Before Cassius came along, athletes were basically quiet. They just went about their jobs, and they didn't boast about it or call attention to themselves. I know that sounds strange, since athletes today are often doing

Cassius Clay poses for the camera during a training session at City Parks Gym in New York.

end zone dances or telling interviewers how fabulous they are. But back then, it wasn't done—until Cassius Clay came along. Some people didn't like his cockiness. Others loved his showmanship. But love him or hate him, everyone knew who he was.

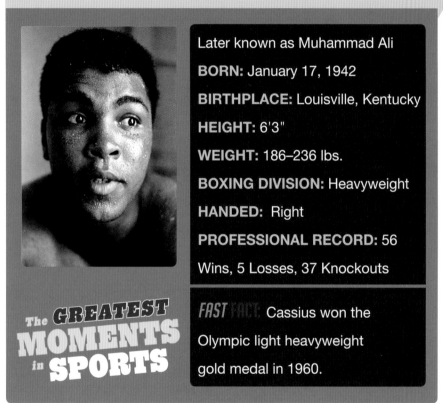

CASSIUS MARCELLUS CLAY JR.

Later known as Muhammad Ali

BORN: January 17, 1942

BIRTHPLACE: Louisville, Kentucky

HEIGHT: 6'3"

WEIGHT: 186–236 lbs.

BOXING DIVISION: Heavyweight

HANDED: Right

PROFESSIONAL RECORD: 56 Wins, 5 Losses, 37 Knockouts

The GREATEST MOMENTS in SPORTS

FAST FACT Cassius won the Olympic light heavyweight gold medal in 1960.

Sonny Liston was a very different kind of athlete. He was big and powerful and had very large hands. When he started to box, he would knock everybody out. But while Cassius had a loud and boisterous personality, Liston did not. He was often referred to as surly, not very friendly. And as a result, he wasn't popular.

In 1962, Liston fought Floyd Patterson for the heavyweight championship. Patterson was a likable man, so the fight was set up as "good guy vs. bad guy." And the bad guy won. Liston knocked out Patterson in the first round. He returned home to Philadelphia, where he had been living. He thought the people there would make a big deal of his becoming a world champion. They didn't. There was no ceremony, no fuss. He and Patterson staged a rematch in 1963. Same fighters, same result. Liston knocked him out again in the first round. Liston was champion, but he wasn't liked very much. And that set up a fascinating championship fight the next year.

What a matchup it was. It took place in Miami Beach, Florida, on February 25, 1964. Cassius was just 21 years old. Nobody knew exactly how old Liston was. He could have been as old as 35. Throughout the time leading up to the fight, Cassius would taunt Liston by calling him lots of names, including "big ugly bear." Cassius would boast that he would "float like a butterfly and sting like a bee." Everyone knew that Liston was the more powerful boxer, but Cassius would say "your hands can't hit what your eyes can't see." As popular as Cassius was, there were many sports fans who were hoping that Liston would "shut him up."

HEAVYWEIGHT CHAMPION

1964–1967
1974–1978
1978–1979

Cassius Clay shouts "I am the greatest!" after defeating Sonny Liston.

Cassius had never lost as a pro—he was 21 and 0. And he was a few inches taller than Liston. But nobody gave Cassius much of a chance. In a poll of the top sportswriters, nearly every single one of them predicted that Liston would win the fight. And fight fans must have thought so too. The arena was half-empty for one of the most startling fights in boxing history. Cassius had other ideas. He yelled at anyone who would listen that he would win the heavyweight championship of the world. And he even predicted the round he would win, something that boxers never did. He crowed that he "would win in round 8 to prove I am great."

KNOCKOUTS (KO) AND TECHNICAL KNOCKOUTS (TKO)

OPPONENT	TYPE	DATE
Herb Siler	KO	12/27/1960
Jimmy Robinson	KO	02/07/1961
LaMar Clark	KO	04/19/1961
Alejandro Lavorante	KO	07/20/1962
Charlie Powell	KO	01/24/1963
Sonny Liston	**KO**	**05/25/1965**
Brian London	KO	08/06/1966
Zora Folley	KO	03/22/1967
Jürgen Blin	KO	12/26/1971
Bob Foster	KO	11/21/1972
George Foreman	KO	10/30/1974
Jean-Pierre Coopman	KO	02/20/1976
Tony Esperti	TKO	01/17/1961
Donnie Fleeman	TKO	02/21/1961
Alex Miteff	TKO	10/07/1961
Willi Besmanoff	TKO	11/29/1961
Sonny Banks	TKO	02/10/1962
Don Warner	TKO	02/28/1962
George Logan	TKO	04/23/1962
Billy Daniels	TKO	05/19/1962
Archie Moore	TKO	11/15/1962
Henry Cooper	TKO	06/18/1963
Sonny Liston	**TKO**	**02/25/1964**
Floyd Patterson	TKO	11/22/1965
Henry Cooper	TKO	05/21/1966
Karl Mildenberger	TKO	09/10/1966
Cleveland Williams	TKO	11/14/1966
Jerry Quarry	TKO	10/26/1970
Oscar Bonavena	TKO	12/07/1970
Jimmy Ellis	TKO	07/26/1971
Jerry Quarry	TKO	06/27/1972
Alvin Lewis	TKO	07/19/1972
Floyd Patterson	TKO	09/20/1972
Chuck Wepner	TKO	03/24/1975
Ron Lyle	TKO	05/16/1975
Joe Frazier	TKO	10/01/1975
Richard Dunn	TKO	05/24/1976

Clay predicts he will win in eight rounds against Liston.

On March 6, 1964, Cassius Clay adopts his new name, **MUHAMMAD ALI**, which means "praiseworthy one."

was, Cassius was having problems. And if you can't see in a boxing ring, that's a big problem. But Cassius's trainer washed out Cassius's eyes and sent his fighter back out for the fifth round. By now, his eyes were clearing up, and he continued his assault on Liston.

At the end of the sixth round, something amazing happened. Liston just sat on his stool and didn't get up. He didn't answer the bell for the seventh round. He said his shoulder hurt so bad that he couldn't continue the fight. It was over. Cassius had stunned everyone and had become the heavyweight champion of the world. He ran into the ring and did a little dance. Then, he jumped onto the ropes and started screaming at the sportswriters that he had told them so. He yelled, "I am the greatest!"

And then the bell rang. Liston came out determined to put Cassius on his back, but Cassius, being faster and quicker than the slow and plodding Liston, jabbed, danced, and survived the first round. By the third round, Cassius had opened a cut under Liston's eye. "Big bad" Sonny Liston no longer looked unbeatable.

But in the fourth round, Cassius suddenly had trouble seeing. His eyes were burning. They guessed it came from Liston's gloves. Maybe it was a substance that was being used to stop the bleeding under Liston's eye. Whatever it

Cassius beat Liston again in the rematch the following year and went on to box for another 17 years. Along the way, he became the first man to ever win the heavyweight championship three different times. And he also became a beloved sports figure, dedicating his life to doing good for others. He has received virtually every award a man can get, including the Presidential Medal of Freedom. He has also been voted the "Sportsman of the Century" by *Sports Illustrated* in the United States, and by the BBC (British Broadcasting Company) in England.

And when the 1996 Olympics began in Atlanta, Georgia, out of all the thousands of American athletes who have ever competed in the Olympics, it was Muhammad Ali who was chosen to light the Olympic flame at the Opening Ceremony. It was Muhammad Ali, then known as Cassius Clay, who proclaimed to the world that "I am the greatest." And you know what? He really was.

"Everyone predicted that Sonny Liston would destroy me. And he was scary. But it's lack of faith that makes people afraid of meeting challenges, and I believed in myself."

–MUHAMMAD ALI

WILT
SCORES
100

There are a handful of athletes who are truly "larger than life." Wilt Chamberlain is definitely one of them. In fact, nobody was "larger" than Wilt in so many ways. He stood 7 foot 1 tall, and at times in his career, his weight exceeded 300 pounds. And to say that he was legendary doesn't even begin to scratch the surface.

He used to say "nobody loves Goliath," meaning that people root for the little guy, never the big guy. But I loved Wilt. He had a hearty laugh to match his size. When my young son asked Wilt how he could drive a car, Wilt joked that he didn't fit in any car, so he sits with the driver's side door open and pushes along the ground with his foot, as though he's riding a scooter. And then he let out one of his belly laughs. There are a million stories about Wilt, and most of them sound like exaggerations, but they are not. Okay, the car story was, but the story of the night he scored 100 points in an NBA game is absolutely true.

If you look in the NBA record book, you'll lose count of how many times the name Wilt Chamberlain appears. He holds the record for most games scoring 50 or more points. He holds the record for highest scoring average by a rookie and the record for highest field goal percentage in a season. He holds just about every rebounding record, including most rebounds in a single game (55). Have you ever heard of a triple-double? That's where a player scores at least 10 points, grabs 10 rebounds, and dishes out 10 assists in the same game. Wilt is the only player to ever score a *double* triple-double. In a game in 1968 against Detroit, he scored 22 points, had 25 rebounds, and 21 assists!

There was never anyone like him. The NBA had to change all sorts of rules because of Wilt. They made the lane under the basket wider. They created the defensive goaltending rule, which prevents a player from blocking a shot as it is coming down toward the basket. You can only block it when the ball is on the way up. They even changed the foul-shooting rules because of him. Wilt would leap from behind the foul line and drop the ball in the basket before he hit the floor. Because of him, a player has to stay behind the foul line when he shoots. The records and the rule changes are amazing, but there was never a night quite like March 2, 1962, in Hershey, Pennsylvania.

The Philadelphia Warriors (now known as the Golden State Warriors) were trying to attract new fans, so they played some of their games in the tiny town of Hershey, Pennsylvania. Hershey, of course, is best known as the home of the Hershey chocolate factory. But on a Friday night in March, about 4,000 fans showed up at the half-empty Hersheypark Arena. Many of them didn't even come to watch the basketball game between the Warriors

Wilt Chamberlain attacks the basket against the New York Knicks.

and the New York Knicks. Lots of fans came to see the preliminary game, which was an exhibition basketball game between some NFL players from the Philadelphia Eagles and the Baltimore Colts. Those who stayed afterward to watch the Warriors and the Knicks didn't realize they were about to see the most famous thing to happen in Hershey since the chocolate bar.

The Knicks were undermanned that night. Their starting center Phil Jordan was out with an injury, so replacing him was Darrall Imhoff, who certainly wasn't in the same league as "Wilt the Stilt." Then again, almost nobody was.

The game was lopsided from the beginning. The Warriors took an early lead and never gave it up. After one quarter, they led by 16 points, 42–26. Of those 42 points, Wilt scored 23. By halftime, the Philadelphia lead was 11, but Wilt's point total had now grown to 41. And still nobody thought too much of it. Wilt had had plenty of big games before, so fans and players didn't have "100 points" on their minds. Wilt had set the record for most points in a game by scoring 78 earlier that season, and he still had a long way to go until he could reach that mark.

As the third quarter began, the Warriors kept passing the ball to Wilt, and he kept scoring. When the quarter ended, they had built their lead to 125–104. Wilt had

WILTON "WILT" CHAMBERLAIN

BORN: August 21, 1936

BIRTHPLACE: Philadelphia, Pennsylvania

HEIGHT: 7'1"   **WEIGHT:** 275 lbs.

TEAM: Philadelphia Warriors (1959–1962); San Francisco Warriors (1962–1964); Philadelphia 76ers (1964–1968); L.A. Lakers (1968–1973)

POSITION: Center

NUMBER: 13

The GREATEST MOMENTS in SPORTS

FAST FACT: Wilt led the league in the most points per game for 7 straight seasons (1959–1966).

Wilt Chamberlain had some great nicknames, including **WILT THE STILT** and **THE BIG DIPPER**.

scored 28 points in the quarter and now had 69 for the game. His record of 78 was within reach.

And he made it easily. A little over four minutes into the fourth quarter, he had scored his record-breaking

Wilt Chamberlain holds a sign with the number of points he scored against New York on March 2, 1962.

DARRALL IMHOFF is forever linked to Wilt in sports history as the man who played defense while Wilt scored 100 points in one game.

79th point. The fans went crazy. They started screaming: "Give it to Wilt!" "Give it to Wilt!" And the Warriors did.

As Wilt got closer to 100 points, things got a little wacky. The Knicks didn't want to be known as the team that allowed a player to score 100 points, so they would intentionally foul other Warrior players so Wilt couldn't score. The Warriors countered by fouling the Knicks on purpose so they could get the ball back. And while all this was going on, Wilt continued to pile up points. His total stood at 98 with less than a minute to go. It looked like the entire Knicks team was guarding Wilt. They really didn't want him to get 100. Wilt went near the basket. They passed him the ball, but he missed the shot. His teammate got the rebound and passed it back to Wilt. But he missed again. And again the Warriors got the rebound. This time, they passed the ball high to Chamberlain and he dunked it home! He had done it. He had scored an incredible 100 points in a single game.

The game wasn't on television, so there is no video of Wilt's amazing night. But the game was heard on the radio, and Bill Campbell was calling the play-by-play on WCAU radio. With 46 seconds to go, when Wilt dunked the ball to make it an even 100 points, Campbell excitedly made this call: "He made it, he made it, he made it, a dipper dunk, he made it!" Then, Campbell described how the fans were running out onto the court and the officials had to stop the game.

LISTEN to this **MOMENT** TRACK 7

When they finished the game, the numbers were amazing. Philadelphia had beaten the Knicks 169–147. Wilt had taken 63 shots and made 36 of them. Wilt was known to be a horrible foul shooter. During the course of his career, he barely made half of his free throws. But that night in Hershey, he made an astounding 28 of 32 from the line. Wilt not only set the record for most points in the game, but he also set records for most shots taken (63), most shots made (36), most free throws made (28), most points in a quarter (31), and most points in a half (59).

Fans might have come to Hershey to watch some football players scrimmage in a basketball game, but what they got to see was simply amazing. The truth is, nobody is likely to score 100 points again in a single game ever. Then again, we probably will never see another player quite like "Wilt the Stilt" Chamberlain.

WILT CHAMBERLAIN'S NBA RECORDS

Wilt holds 72 different NBA records, so we don't have room to list them all. But here are a few:

Wilt Chamberlain shows off his skills during a workout.

- Most points in a single game: 100
- Most points in a rookie season: 2,707
- Most games in a career with 50 or more points: 118
- Most field goals in one game: 36
- Most rebounds in a single game: 55
- Most rebounds in a career: 23,924

MICHAEL JORDAN'S SHOT

H ere's one of the things that fascinates me about sports: When you get to the pros, you have the greatest athletes who play that sport—they're the best of the best. But Michael Jordan wasn't simply the best pro of all of them—he was light years better. Few people predicted it when he first began playing, and yet he is now considered by most to be the greatest basketball player of all time.

When Michael was a freshman at North Carolina in 1981, he averaged around 13 points a game, which was good but not extraordinary. In his sophomore year, North Carolina made it to the national championship game, where the Tar Heels played Georgetown, led by the great future Hall of Fame center Patrick Ewing. North Carolina trailed by one point with 17 seconds to go. They got the ball to Michael on the left side and—swish! North Carolina took the lead and won the NCAA championship. What kid doesn't dream about winning the biggest game of the year? Michael had done it. And it wouldn't be the last time.

When he left North Carolina, he was considered a terrific player offensively and defensively, but nobody could have predicted what he would accomplish in his career. In fact, he wasn't the first pick in the NBA draft. Two teams had passed over the future superstar before he was drafted by the Chicago Bulls.

Michael Jordan dunks and wins the slam-dunk competition during the 1988 All-Star weekend.

Michael Jordan flies past Toronto Raptors guard Alvin Robertson.

Michael **AIR** Jordan holds the NBA record for career average for points per game.

But it didn't take long for the world to take notice of Michael's talent. Just one month into his rookie season in 1984, *Sports Illustrated* magazine put a picture of Michael on the cover with the headline: "A Star Is Born." He went on to average 28 points a game, and he had done it against the very best players in the world. He was voted to the All-Star Game and named Rookie of the Year. Not a bad start to his pro career.

The Chicago Bulls made the playoffs his rookie year, but they got bounced in the first round by Milwaukee.

In Michael's second year, the Bulls played the Boston Celtics in the first round of the playoffs. Boston beat the Bulls in three straight games and would go on to win the NBA championship. But in Game 2, the young Michael revealed what the future would hold. He scored an NBA playoff record of 63 points. It was one of the greatest playoff performances the NBA had ever seen.

The next year, he continued to do amazing things. He went wild offensively, leading the league with 37 points a game. And defensively, he became the first player to ever block 200 shots and make 100 steals in the same season. And yet, when the playoffs came around, the Bulls again were swept away by Boston.

As each year went by, he did more amazing things. In 1988, he won both the MVP and the Defensive Player of the Year award. And again, no championship—the Bulls lost in the second round to Detroit.

In 1989, Michael made another amazing shot. In the second round of the playoffs, the Bulls were playing Cleveland. It all game down to a fifth deciding game. And that game came down to one shot. The Bulls were trailing the Cavaliers 100–99 when they got the ball to Michael. His jump shot from the foul-line area was good at the buzzer! Michael leaped into the air, pumping his fist. He was mobbed by his teammates. They had won the game, 101–100.

Michael Jordan holds his fifth MVP trophy.

Michael Jordan was named the NBA's Most Valuable Player five times:

- 1987–88
- 1990–91
- 1991–92
- 1995–96
- 1997–98

He was also named the MVP for the NBA Finals six times!

It was another game-winning shot for Michael, but still no championship. For the second year in a row, they were beaten by Detroit. And then the Pistons beat them again the next season. A pattern had developed. Michael would do amazing things in the regular season and even in the playoffs, but every year, the Bulls had come up short for the championship—until 1991.

In 1991, the Bulls finally beat Detroit; in fact, they swept them four games to none. There was one more hurdle: the Los Angeles Lakers, starring Magic Johnson. Michael had another incredible moment in Game 2. At one point, he had made 13 consecutive field goals. The 13th is one of the greatest basketball highlights of all time. Michael went up in the air to dunk with the ball in his right hand. As the defender came to meet him, he switched the ball to his left hand in midair and laid the ball into the basket. It was one of the most amazing baskets ever. The Bulls went on to win the NBA championship in five games, Michael's first. Of course, he was named the MVP of the Finals.

And what did Michael and the Bulls do for an encore? They won the NBA championship the next two years.

And then, Michael retired. He said he had lost his desire to play. He got it back a year and a half later, but when the playoffs came along, the Bulls were beaten by Shaquille O'Neal and Orlando. But the next year, Michael and the Bulls started another championship run. He won his fourth NBA title and then his fifth. And that set up the 1997–1998 play-offs and another amazing shot.

That year, the Bulls played the Utah Jazz in the NBA Finals. Chicago was leading three games to two when they traveled to Utah on June 14, 1998. Another win, and they would clinch their third straight NBA title and their sixth in eight years. As time wound down in the game, Chicago was trailing

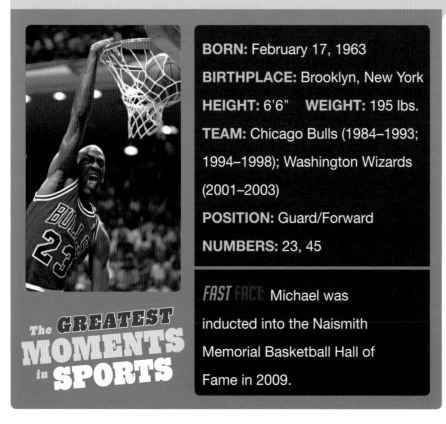

MICHAEL JEFFERY JORDAN

BORN: February 17, 1963

BIRTHPLACE: Brooklyn, New York

HEIGHT: 6'6"   **WEIGHT:** 195 lbs.

TEAM: Chicago Bulls (1984–1993; 1994–1998); Washington Wizards (2001–2003)

POSITION: Guard/Forward

NUMBERS: 23, 45

FAST FACT: Michael was inducted into the Naismith Memorial Basketball Hall of Fame in 2009.

The GREATEST MOMENTS in SPORTS

Michael Jordan launches one of his famous jump shots.

over to Malone and slapped the ball out of his hands. He stole the ball!

Time was running out in the game, and as Michael neared the foul line, he started to dribble to his right, with Bryon Russell of the Jazz guarding him. Suddenly, Michael crossed over his dribble to the left and let fly. And just like at North Carolina in 1982, and just like against Cleveland nine years earlier, the shot was good to win the game. Only this time, it won the NBA championship.

LISTEN *to this* **MOMENT** **TRACK 8**

Again, just as he had done when he won the series against Cleveland, when the clock struck zero, he jumped into the air and pumped his fist. He then held up five fingers on his left hand, and one on his right. He had just won his incredible sixth NBA championship. And in all six Finals, he was voted the MVP. He was not just the best basketball player in the league, but the best by a huge margin. He could do it all—score, defend, and, most important, when his team needed a basket, he delivered. No wonder he's considered the best basketball player who ever lived.

86–83 with 40 seconds left. Of course, the Bulls gave Michael the ball, and with two Jazz players trying to stop him, he scored a layup to cut the deficit to 86–85. Now Utah had the ball, and they passed it to their great forward, Karl Malone. What did Michael do? He just ran

VILLANOVA
VS.
GEORGETOWN

There's a reason they call the NCAA basketball tournament March Madness. Just look at 1957. In the semifinal game, North Carolina had to go three overtimes to beat Michigan State. And just 24 hours later, they had to go up against Kansas, led by the incredible Wilt Chamberlain. And North Carolina won again—and again, it took three overtimes. What are the odds of that? And then there was the 1985 final in Kentucky. It took place on April Fool's Day, and boy were the experts fooled!

Georgetown was the best college basketball team in the country. They had made it to the NCAA finals in 1982, won the championship in 1984, and were having a great year so far in 1985. They were led by the amazing Patrick Ewing, who would go on to become the first draft pick of the New York Knicks later that year.

During the season, they played St. John's at Madison Square Garden. There was a great deal of excitement nationwide over that game. It was number one playing number two in college basketball, and Georgetown won. The two teams met up again for the Big East championship game, also at Madison Square Garden. Georgetown won again! And when it came to the 1985 NCAA tournament semifinals, Georgetown played St. John's a third time that year. And for a third time, Georgetown beat them.

Georgetown had rolled through the very tough Big East conference. But they weren't a very popular team. The Georgetown Hoyas had an aura about them. They were big and tough. Some thought they were bullies, so many sports fans rooted against them. Whether people liked them or not, in 1985, they were driving toward another championship. And it looked like nobody could beat them, certainly not Villanova.

The Villanova Wildcats didn't strike fear in anybody. They were a pretty good team but not great. During the regular season, they had just a 9–7 record in the Big East conference. Nothing special. They certainly were not in the same "league" as Georgetown, which had a 14–2 conference record. But somehow, Villanova kept winning when it counted the most.

And there they were, Georgetown and Villanova. Two teams from the same conference still standing at the end, ready to play for the 1985 NCAA championship.

They had already met twice that season, and Georgetown won both games. Nobody gave Villanova a chance. I mean nobody. One sportswriter in Kentucky wrote that the matchup between Georgetown and Villanova was so unfair, they shouldn't even bother playing it. Who could beat Georgetown? They were the defending champions. What had Villanova done?

And then they played the game.

Georgetown was the complete package. In addition to Ewing, Coach John Thompson had two other future NBA players on his roster: Reggie Williams and David Wingate. Not only could they score points, but their defense was awesome. They held opponents to under 40 percent shooting. That was the best in the country. And they dominated on the boards, out-rebounding their opposition by a wide margin. Some basketball experts think the 1985 Georgetown Hoyas rank up amongst the greatest college basketball teams of all time.

Villanova? They arrived at the final game having lost 10 games. While Georgetown had three stars on the team, the Wildcats had just one. He was 6 foot 9 inch center Ed Pinckney. And he had to go up against Ewing, the three-time All-American center who stood 7 feet tall. But what Villanova did better than any other team was play scrappy defense. They held opponents to under 60 points. And even though they had lost to Georgetown twice during the season, the Hoyas had trouble scoring. In fact, Villanova was the only team to hold Georgetown under 60 all season.

One more thing worth noting: the shot clock wasn't introduced until the following season in college basketball. So, Villanova could hold on to the ball for long periods of time on offense. Their strategy was very simple: Take your time on offense and look for the good shot. And on defense? Play the same tough stingy game they had played all season. Before the game, their coach, Rollie Massimino, told his team to picture themselves winning the game. As it turned out, they did a lot better than that.

Patrick Ewing (No. 33) from Georgetown defends Harold Pressley (No. 21) from Villanova.

As the first half unfolded, things were going Georgetown's way. Midway through the half, Williams hit three straight shots for the Hoyas, and Georgetown took an 18–12 lead. But Villanova fought back. As the first half was nearing an end, Villanova had the ball, trailing by one point. Then, they went into a stall. They held on to the ball for nearly two minutes. With the clock winding down on the half, Harold Pressley went up over Ewing and scored. The Wildcats, huge underdogs, had themselves a halftime lead, 29–28.

The second half was one for the record books. It's often referred to as a "perfect" half of basketball. Well, it was almost perfect—Villanova missed one shot in the entire second half. Just one. The lead changed hands several times. Villanova at one point led by 5, but Georgetown regained the lead. With about two-and-a-half minutes to go in the game, Villanova's Harold Jensen calmly swished a wide-open jump shot from the right side. The Wildcats had retaken the lead, 55–54. They would never trail again.

Down the stretch, they kept going to the foul line and they kept hitting their free throws. When it was over, the numbers were eye-popping. They had missed only six shots the entire game and only five free throws. They had shot an incredible 78.6 percent from the field that night, an all-time record. And, remember, Georgetown had held their opponents to under 40 percent shooting.

Ed Pinckney (No. 54) and his Villanova teammates celebrate their victory over Georgetown.

The final score was Villanova 66, Georgetown 64. Sports fans were stunned. The Wildcats had pulled off one of the greatest upsets in the history of sports. And it wasn't just lucky, or fluky. It wasn't some "Hail Mary" pass or fortunate bounce. They had played a nearly flawless basketball game to beat the defending champions. After the final buzzer, the Villanova players and coaches hugged each other with tears in their eyes. They were NCAA basketball champions.

Coach Rollie Massimino called it a miracle.

RICHARD PETTY

You've read about some great nicknames in these pages. Muhammad Ali is "the Greatest" and Wayne Gretzky is "the Great One." And then there's Richard Petty. He was simply "the King." There's never been a race-car driver quite like him. The numbers kind of tell the story. He began driving in NASCAR when he was 21 years old, and over the next 34 years, he piled up victories as if they were used tires. Would you believe he won 200 races? Nobody else has come close, and it's unlikely that anyone ever will. Along the way, he won the biggest race in the world, the Daytona 500, seven times. Nobody has done that. But as I said, the numbers "kind of" tell the story. Let me start at the beginning.

Richard's dad Lee was also a driver. He won the very first Daytona 500 in 1959. In the sport of auto racing, the kids of famous drivers often become drivers too. In fact, at one point, there were four generations of race-car drivers in the Petty family.

Richard appeared on the scene in July 1958 in a race in Toronto. He finished 17th. It was hardly a smashing debut. Before the next year was out, he had finished in the top 10 nine different times. He didn't win a single race, and yet, he was named Rookie of the Year. During the 1960 season, he won three times. And he kept winning. In 1964, he won the big one, the race his father had won five years earlier, the Daytona 500. He led for nearly the entire 200 laps of the race, and he won it by a large margin. Two years later, he won it again, becoming the first to ever win "the Great American Race" twice. But that was nothing compared with what was to come.

The year was 1967. He entered 48 races, which means that he raced just about every week. In those 48 races, he won an astounding 27 times! And from August to October, he won every single week. He won a record 10 straight races. It was one of the most amazing winning streaks in any sport. Experts say it's a record that will never be broken. And that's when he got the nickname "the King." That's what he truly was.

Richard Petty celebrates his 200th NASCAR win.

In 1970, Richard Petty won 20 races, including his third Daytona 500. He became the first race-car driver to collect more than $1,000,000 in career earnings.

By the time he got back onto the track, he was trailing by 10 laps. It didn't look good, but "King Richard" kept making up ground. And he went on to win the race by five laps!

As the years went by, he kept piling up the wins, and some interesting events occurred along the way. The 1976 Daytona 500 was pretty weird. Richard was battling David Pearson when their bumpers hit. Both cars spun out and hit the wall. Richard said he thought he would spin right across the finish line and win the race with the car facing backward. But Richard's car stalled out about 20 yards from the finish line, and he couldn't get it restarted. Pearson was able to get his car moving to the finish line and won the race. Richard finished second. If not for that mishap, Richard might have won the Daytona 500 eight times.

There were a couple of other wacky Daytona 500s for "the King." In 1979, there was no way he was going to win. Donnie Allison and Cale Yarborough were fighting for the lead and would continue to fight after the race was over. The two cars crashed on the final lap, and that allowed Richard to win a very close finish for yet another Daytona 500 win. After the race, Allison and Yarborough got into a fistfight. That crazy race is credited for being the springboard for NASCAR, helping

And, of course, he won the driving championship that year (one of seven times he did it).

What made Richard so good? There are a lot of great drivers out on the circuit, but Richard was smart, drove hard, and never gave up. One race summed it up. It was in Nashville in July of that magical year of 1967. He was leading the race when one of his tires blew out, and his car smashed up against the wall. He was somehow able to drive his car into the pits, where his crew changed the tires and hammered the metal on his car back into place.

to make it the popular sport it has become. And, naturally, Richard had won it.

In 1981, it wasn't luck for Richard that helped him win; it was race smarts. As the Daytona 500 was winding down, all the leaders had to make a pit stop for fuel and tires. That is, all of the leaders except for Richard. While the other drivers stopped and got a refill along with tire changes, Richard only stopped for fuel. He and his crew thought his tires were just fine. And it turns out they were right. Those precious seconds that they saved by not having to change his tires propelled Richard into the lead. He was first across the finish line with his seventh and final Daytona 500 win.

There was one huge milestone yet to come. It was the Fourth of July, 1984, at the Firecracker 400 at the Daytona International Speedway. Richard came into the race with an astounding 199 career wins. President Ronald Reagan was on hand to watch. It was the first time a sitting President of the United States had ever attended a NASCAR race. And, fittingly enough, the President and everyone else saw a race of historic proportions. It all came down to Richard and Cale Yarborough. And "the King" did it. He won the race by inches, his 200th career win. And celebrating in the winner's circle were a "King" and a President. It was an amazing milestone for Richard. For one thing,

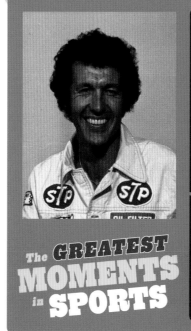

RICHARD PETTY, "THE KING"

BORN: July 2, 1937

BIRTHPLACE: Level Cross, North Carolina

RACING TEAM: Richard Petty Motorsports

CAR NUMBER: 43

The **GREATEST MOMENTS** *in* **SPORTS**

FAST FACT: Richard was voted Nascar's Most Popular Driver nine times (1962, 1964, 1968, 1970, 1974, 1975, 1976, 1977, and 1978.

it was the last win of his Hall of Fame career. But how impressive is 200 wins? The guy in second place, David Pearson, has "only" 105.

Eight years later, Richard got to spend some time with another president, George H. W. Bush. The President presented "the King" with the Medal of Freedom. Richard Petty became the first motorsports athlete to ever be honored with the award.

So, add up the numbers: 200 wins, seven Daytona 500s, and millions in earnings. Not to mention the awards and worldwide adulation. It all adds up to a most phenomenal racing career. A career fit for a "King."

U.S. WOMEN'S WORLD CUP SOCCER

f you're a sports fan, you probably think that your favorite sport has been around forever. Of course, that's not true. You'd be surprised to know how new some of the sports are. Women's team sports are really new. For example, if you like college basketball, the NCAA men's championship has been competed since 1939. But the women's tournament has only been around since 1982.

Soccer is the most popular sport in the world. It's really the only sport that people play in every country. There probably isn't a kid on Earth who hasn't played soccer. And the biggest soccer tournament on Earth is called the World Cup. It's the Olympics of soccer. They have it every four years. The men staged their first World Cup in 1930 in Uruguay. The U.S. team finished third. It remains its best-ever World Cup finish.

The first women's World Cup wasn't held until 1991 in China. It was a different story for the American women. They won that first tournament by beating Norway 2–1 in the final. But even though it was the first World Cup championship in U.S. soccer history, not a lot of Americans took notice. That was about to change.

Role models in sports are much easier to come by for boys. They've got baseball, football, basketball, and hockey, not to mention boxing and any other sport you can think of. But for girls, it was limited. There were tennis stars like Billie Jean King and Chris Evert. And there were Olympic athletes in track, gymnastics, and figure skating. But there weren't many in team sports.

And then the Olympics came to America in 1996. For men's soccer, the World Cup was the major competition, not the Olympics. But for women's soccer, the World Cup was fairly new, so many Americans paid attention to the sport for the first time at the Olympics.

THE 1999 UNITED STATES WOMEN'S SOCCER TEAM

NO.	NAME	POSITION
1	Briana Scurry	GK
2	Lorrie Fair	DF
3	Christie Rampone	DF
4	Carla Overbeck	DF
5	Tiffany Roberts	MF
6	Brandi Chastain	MF
7	Sara Whalen	DF
8	Shannon MacMillan	FW
9	Mia Hamm	FW
10	Michelle Akers	MF
11	Julie Foudy	MF
12	Cindy Parlow	MF
13	Kristine Lilly	FW
14	Joy Fawcett	DF
15	Tisha Venturini	MF
16	Tiffeny Milbrett	FW
17	Danielle Fotopoulos	FW
18	Saskia Webber	GK
19	Tracy Ducar	GK
20	Kate Markgraf	DF

Coach: Tony DiCicco

The 1996 Summer Olympics were held in Atlanta, Georgia. This was the first time women's soccer was added to the program.

The final was played at the University of Georgia in Athens, and it drew an amazing crowd of over 76,000 fans. It was the largest crowd to ever see a women's soccer game. The United States beat China 2–1 to win the first-ever Olympic gold medal in women's soccer. But that was just the beginning. Few predicted what would happen three years later when America hosted the third Women's World Cup.

Entering the 1999 World Cup, the U.S. team certainly had some star players. The most prominent was the incomparable Mia Hamm. Mia was the youngest person to ever play for the U.S. National Team in 1987 when she was just 15 years old. Mia was dynamic. She would slash her way down the field and score goals in bunches. She would become the greatest goal scorer in soccer history. She was a member of that gold medal–winning team in 1996, and *People* magazine named her one of the "50 Most Beautiful People" in 1997. Mia was a star.

What Mia was to the offense, Joy Fawcett was to the defense. Many thought she was the best defender in the world. She could do it all, even score goals. Brandi Chastain also played defense, and she wound up scoring the most famous goal in the history of women's soccer.

Mia Hamm (No. 9) defends a kick by China's Jie Bol (No. 14) during the World Cup finals.

MIA HAMM

BORN: March 17, 1972

BIRTHPLACE: Selma, Alabama

HEIGHT: 5'5"   **WEIGHT:** 125 lbs.

TEAM: U.S. Women's National Team (1987–2004); Washington Freedom (2001–2003)

POSITION: Forward

FAST FACT At 15 years old, Mia was the youngest player to ever play for the U.S. National Soccer Team.

The GREATEST MOMENTS in SPORTS

The tournament began, and for the first time, it was held in the United States. The Americans breezed through its early games. They beat Denmark 3–0, then Nigeria 7–1, and finally Korea 3–0 in round-robin play. The games were played in front of huge crowds in New Jersey, Chicago, and Foxboro. Along the way, Mia scored two goals. Up next: the single elimination.

In the quarterfinals, the United States played against Germany in Landover, Maryland. The game started poorly for the Americans. Brandi kicked a ball into her own net by mistake. It counted as a goal for Germany, and the Germans

MIA'S ACCOMPLISHMENTS

- 4 NCAA championships (North Carolina)
- 2 World Cup titles
- 2 Olympic Gold medals
- Most international goals scored (man or woman): 158
- Inducted into the National Soccer Hall of Fame in 1997

led 2–1 at halftime. But the United States came back. Tied at 2, Fawcett headed home the winning goal and sent the Americans into the semifinals, where Brazil awaited.

The semifinal game was played at Stanford University in Palo Alto, California, on the Fourth of July. It was certainly a red, white, and blue day for the Americans. Goaltender Briana Scurry was unbeatable. The United States shut out the Brazilians 2–0. And now it was on to the finals and a date with China.

On July 10, 1999, a record crowd of over 90,000 fans, which included President Bill Clinton, jammed the Rose Bowl in Pasadena, California. And what they would see would be historic. It was a tense game throughout. Nobody could score a goal. It was 0–0 after 60 minutes. They played two 15-minute overtime periods. The Chinese came very close to scoring on a couple of occasions, but after 90 minutes of exciting soccer, the score was still 0–0. The World Cup would then be decided on penalty kicks.

Here are the rules for penalty kicks: Each team gets five chances, with the teams alternating shots. The team that scores the most goals wins the game and, in this case, the 1999 World Cup. As the penalty kicks unfolded, China scored its first two kicks and so did the United States, with Fawcett tying the score at 2–2. Then came a critical moment. Liu Ying was up for China. She kicked the ball, and Scurry made the save. The crowd went into a frenzy. Kristine Lilly then gave the United States a 3–2 lead. China tied the score with their next kick, but Mia was up next and gave the United States the lead, 4–3. It was now time for the final two kicks. If Sun Wen didn't score, the United States would win. But Sun Wen scored, and it was all up to Brandi.

One more penalty kick and the United States would win the World Cup. Brandi put the ball down on the grass, took a few steps back, and ran her fingers through her hair. She was ready. A quick approach to the ball. A left-footed kick

BRANDI CHASTAIN

BORN: July 21, 1968

BIRTHPLACE: San Jose, California

HEIGHT: 5'7"   **WEIGHT:** 130 lbs.

TEAM: U.S. Women's National Team (1988–2004); San Jose CyberRays (2001–2003); FC Gold Pride (2009–)

POSITION: Midfielder/Forward

FAST FACT: Brandi played professional soccer in Japan in 1993 and was the team MVP.

The GREATEST MOMENTS in SPORTS

Brandi Chastain defends China's attempt at a shot on goal.

Brandi Chastain celebrates after scoring the game-winning penalty goal against China.

The Chinese media gave the American team's forward line the nickname of "the Triple-Edged Sword."

into the upper-right corner of the goal. She had done it! Brandi had won the World Cup for the United States. She fell to her knees and then did something that the men soccer players do. She pulled off her shirt. She was wearing a black tank top underneath, so it wasn't in any way improper. But it made a huge statement. The women had arrived! She was mobbed and hugged by her teammates as the crowd went wild.

The U.S. women's soccer team had become national heroes. The next day, there was a parade at Disneyland.

They were invited to the White House. They appeared on TV shows and on magazine covers. Little girls everywhere now wanted to play soccer. Male sports stars were often known by one name—Tiger or Babe. And now, for the first time, women soccer players were too—Mia and Brandi. Girls everywhere wanted to be just like them.

BIG RED

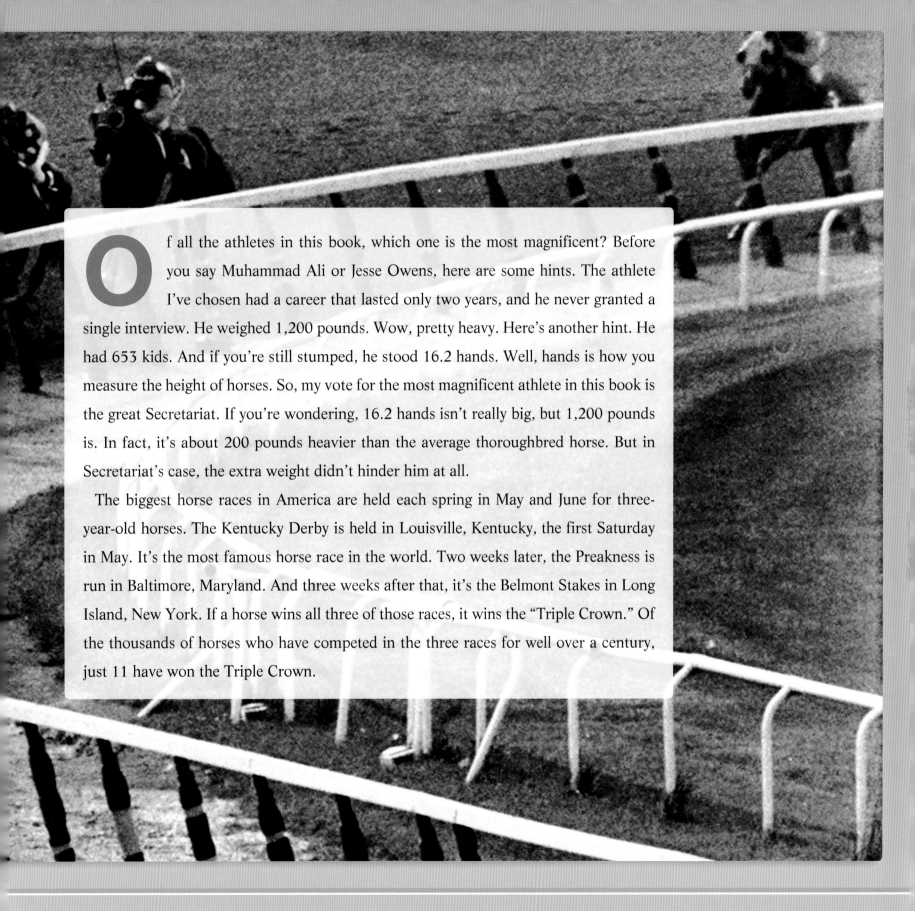

Of all the athletes in this book, which one is the most magnificent? Before you say Muhammad Ali or Jesse Owens, here are some hints. The athlete I've chosen had a career that lasted only two years, and he never granted a single interview. He weighed 1,200 pounds. Wow, pretty heavy. Here's another hint. He had 653 kids. And if you're still stumped, he stood 16.2 hands. Well, hands is how you measure the height of horses. So, my vote for the most magnificent athlete in this book is the great Secretariat. If you're wondering, 16.2 hands isn't really big, but 1,200 pounds is. In fact, it's about 200 pounds heavier than the average thoroughbred horse. But in Secretariat's case, the extra weight didn't hinder him at all.

The biggest horse races in America are held each spring in May and June for three-year-old horses. The Kentucky Derby is held in Louisville, Kentucky, the first Saturday in May. It's the most famous horse race in the world. Two weeks later, the Preakness is run in Baltimore, Maryland. And three weeks after that, it's the Belmont Stakes in Long Island, New York. If a horse wins all three of those races, it wins the "Triple Crown." Of the thousands of horses who have competed in the three races for well over a century, just 11 have won the Triple Crown.

Secretariat was born on March 30, 1970, on a farm in Virginia. He raced for the first time as a two-year-old on July 4, 1972. There were 12 horses in the mile-and-a-quarter race at Aqueduct Racetrack in Queens, New York.

SECRETARIAT, "BIG RED"

BORN: March 30, 1970

BIRTHPLACE: The Meadow Farm in Doswell, Virginia

HEIGHT: 16.2 hands

WEIGHT: 1,200 lbs.

JOCKEY: Ron Turcotte

The GREATEST MOMENTS in SPORTS

FAST FACT: Secretariat was inducted into the National Museum of Racing Hall of Fame in 1974.

Just after the start, he was in tenth place. The big horse charged fast and finished fourth. His owner and trainer were happy. The racing world had no idea what was about to happen. He raced eight more times in 1972 and won seven of those races. He would have won the eighth, but he was disqualified for interfering with another horse. Secretariat was named "Horse of the Year," an extremely rare honor for a two-year-old. But the best was yet to come.

The 99th running of the Kentucky Derby was held on May 14, 1973. A record crowd of over 134,000 fans flocked to famed Churchill Downs to see if Secretariat could live up to his reputation. They had some doubts. He had won his first two races in 1973, but in his final race before the Kentucky Derby, he finished third. So, as 13 horses were loaded into the starting gate for the Kentucky Derby, Secretariat was not a sure thing.

When the race began, his jockey, Ron Turcotte, took his sweet time. Secretariat was in eleventh place, with only two horses behind him. And then, he began to move up. He passed one horse at a time until he was in fifth place. As they neared the final stretch, he kept up his charge, and now there was only one horse between Secretariat and the finish line, Sham. It was no contest. "Big Red" breezed by to capture the Kentucky Derby by two-and-a-half lengths in record time.

The Kentucky Derby is often called "the most exciting two minutes in sports." Not for Secretariat. He became the first horse to run the great race in under two minutes—one minute, 59.4 seconds. It was a record that might never be broken. One down, two to go.

Next up was the Preakness, a shorter race at a mile and 3/16ths. Only five other horses challenged Secretariat that May day at Pimlico Race Course. Could he do it again? This time, Ron Turcotte ran a very different race.

Again, Secretariat started slowly, but almost immediately, he charged from last to first. It's not always smart to do that because horses can tire. But not Secretariat. He never gave up the lead and won the Preakness by

Secretariat and jockey Ron Turcotte race to the finish line to win the Kentucky Derby.

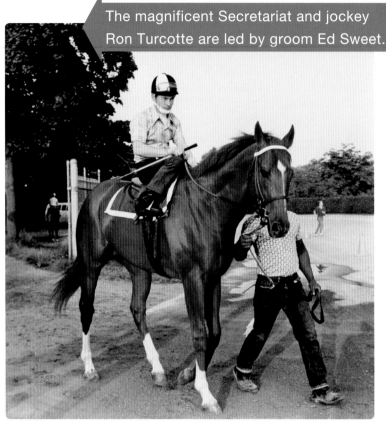

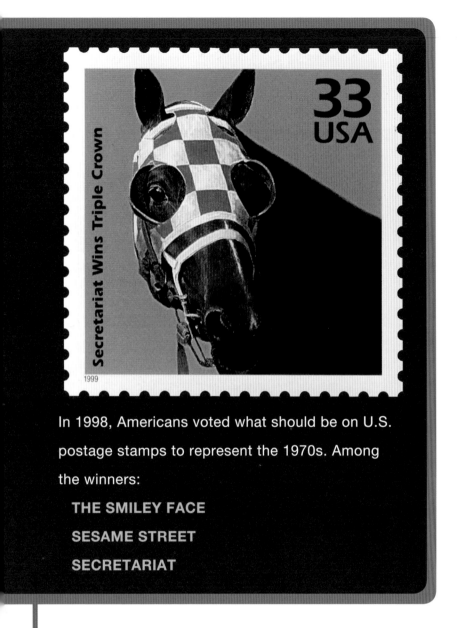

Secretariat Wins Triple Crown

33 USA

1999

In 1998, Americans voted what should be on U.S. postage stamps to represent the 1970s. Among the winners:

THE SMILEY FACE

SESAME STREET

SECRETARIAT

two-and-a-half lengths. The whole country was excited. He had captured the first two jewels of the Triple Crown. He appeared on the covers of major magazines. There was still one race left.

It had been a long 25 years since the last Triple Crown winner, Citation, in 1948. Could Big Red end the drought? The Belmont Stakes. June 9, 1973. This race is a mile and a half, the longest of the Triple Crown races. That's what makes winning the Triple Crown so difficult. You have to win three races in just five weeks. You can have speed for the first two races, but now you need speed and endurance. No wonder they call the Belmont Stakes the "Test of Champions." Well, to say that Secretariat passed the test with flying colors doesn't begin to tell the story.

There were just four horses challenging Secretariat that day, and very early on, it became just a two-horse race between Secretariat and Sham, the horse that finished second in both the Kentucky Derby and the Preakness.

Sham stayed with Secretariat stride for stride for a short while and then Secretariat slowly started to pull away. By a length, two lengths, ten lengths. The gap between Secretariat and the rest of the field just kept growing. Chick Anderson was the track announcer, and at one point, he called out: "Secretariat is all alone. He's out there almost a 16th of a mile away from the rest of the horses." And the lead just kept on growing. Anderson yelled, "He is going to be the Triple Crown Winner…unbelievable…amazing!"

LISTEN *to this* **MOMENT** **TRACK 9**

Secretariat had won the "Test of Champions" by an incredible 31 lengths. He had run the mile and a half in 2 minutes and 24 seconds. That was not only the record at Belmont, but the record for a mile and a half anywhere in the world. Another Secretariat record that will probably never be broken.

He raced six more times after the Belmont Stakes. His last race was October 28, 1973, the Canadian International Stakes in Toronto. Of course, he closed out his career with a win. The final numbers: 21 races, 16 wins, three second-place finishes, and one third-place. Only once in his career did he finish "out of the money," his very first race.

Again in 1973, he was voted "Horse of the Year," but in my book, he's the "Horse of All Time." He was named to various halls of fame and was even honored on a postage stamp. Simply magnificent.

TRIPLE CROWN WINNERS

Secretariat, jockey Ron Turcotte, and groom Ed Sweet pose after winning the Kentucky Derby.

HORSE NAME	JOCKEY	YEAR
Affirmed	Steve Cauthen	1978
Seattle Slew	Jean Cruguet	1977
Secretariat	**Ron Turcotte**	**1973**
Citation	Eddie Arcaro	1948
Assault	Warren Mehrtens	1946
Count Fleet	Johnny Longden	1943
Whirlaway	Eddie Arcaro	1941
War Admiral	Charley Kurtsinger	1937
Omaha	Willie Saunders	1935
Gallant Fox	Earl Sande	1930
Sir Barton	Johnny Loftus	1919

JACKIE ROBINSON

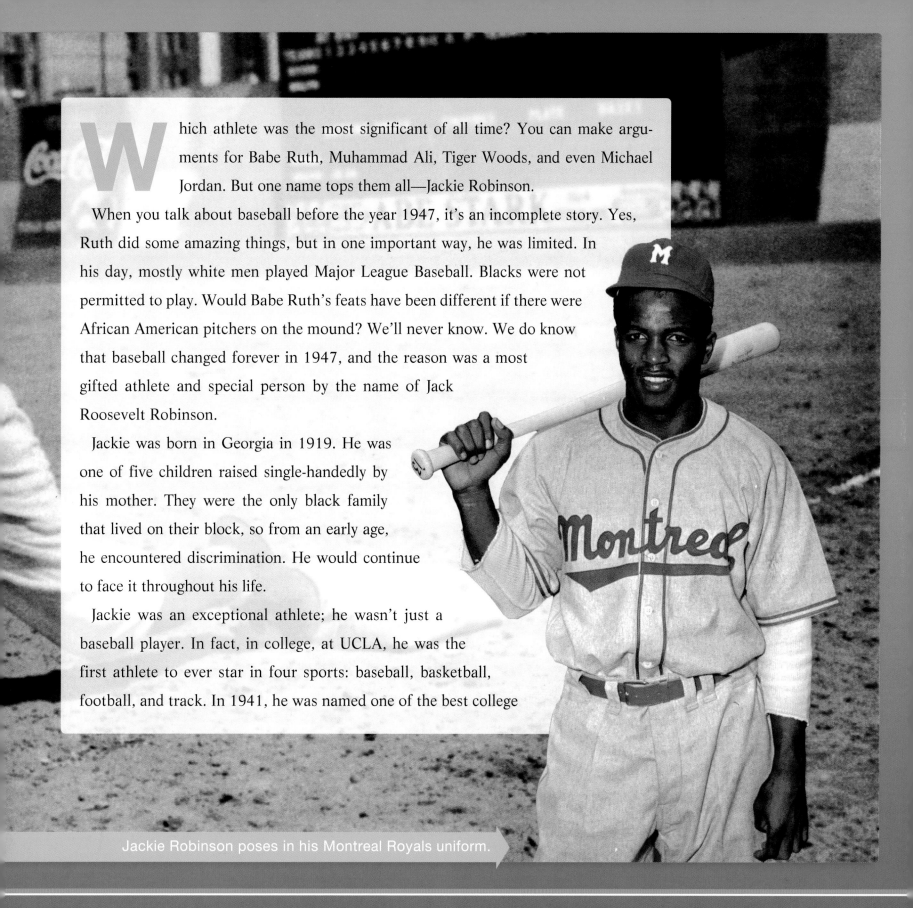

W hich athlete was the most significant of all time? You can make arguments for Babe Ruth, Muhammad Ali, Tiger Woods, and even Michael Jordan. But one name tops them all—Jackie Robinson.

When you talk about baseball before the year 1947, it's an incomplete story. Yes, Ruth did some amazing things, but in one important way, he was limited. In his day, mostly white men played Major League Baseball. Blacks were not permitted to play. Would Babe Ruth's feats have been different if there were African American pitchers on the mound? We'll never know. We do know that baseball changed forever in 1947, and the reason was a most gifted athlete and special person by the name of Jack Roosevelt Robinson.

Jackie was born in Georgia in 1919. He was one of five children raised single-handedly by his mother. They were the only black family that lived on their block, so from an early age, he encountered discrimination. He would continue to face it throughout his life.

Jackie was an exceptional athlete; he wasn't just a baseball player. In fact, in college, at UCLA, he was the first athlete to ever star in four sports: baseball, basketball, football, and track. In 1941, he was named one of the best college

Jackie Robinson poses in his Montreal Royals uniform.

Jackie Robinson, Pee Wee Reese, Willard Marshall, and Johnny Mize before the start of a game on July 2, 1949, in New York City.

football players in the country. He was a fabulous running back. But after college and a stint in the army, he turned his attention to baseball.

In the 1940s, baseball was segregated. The white players played in the major leagues, while black players played in the Negro Leagues. There were teams like the New York Black Yankees and the Homestead (Pennsylvania) Grays. Jackie joined up with the Kansas City Monarchs and in 1945 toured the country. Jackie caught the eye of Brooklyn Dodgers president Branch Rickey. Rickey wanted Jackie to "break the color barrier" of Major League Baseball. Rickey knew that things would be tough for Jackie. Would fans and teammates accept a black man in an all-white sport? Rickey told Jackie that no matter how difficult things got, he should keep his cool. Don't get angry. Don't fight back. It turned out to be great advice. That way, Jackie could concentrate on baseball.

And concentrate he did. In 1946, he had a tremendous year for the Dodgers minor league team, the Montreal Royals. In his very first game against Jersey City, he went 4 for 5, including a three-run homer. He had four runs batted in and four runs scored. He even stole two bases. What a debut! It got better and better. Despite the racial abuse he would hear from the fans, he not only led the league in hitting that year, but he led the Royals to the "Little World Series" championship. He was ready for the big time. But was the big time ready for him?

On April 15, 1947, at Ebbets Field in Brooklyn, Jackie made history. He became the first black to play Major League Baseball. He didn't get a hit that day, but his seventh-inning bunt was a key moment in the game. He wound up scoring the winning run as the Brooklyn Dodgers beat the Boston Braves 5–3.

JACKIE ROBINSON

BORN: January 31, 1919

BIRTHPLACE: Cairo, Georgia

HEIGHT: 5'11"   **WEIGHT:** 204 lbs.

BATTED: Right   **THREW:** Right

POSITION PLAYED: Second Base

TEAM: Kansas City Monarchs (1945); Brooklyn Dodgers (1947–1956)

NUMBER: 42

FAST FACT While in college at UCLA, Jackie was the first ever to be a four-sport letter winner. He played football, track, basketball, and baseball.

The GREATEST MOMENTS in SPORTS

Baseball was the easy part for Jackie. Off the field, things were difficult. Fans yelled racial insults. The Dodgers were afraid that the opposing pitcher would throw the ball at him. Even some of his own teammates had threatened to go on strike if Jackie took the field. A baseball memorabilia collector once showed me a special baseball cap that Jackie wore when he batted. It was before the era of batting helmets. Jackie had inserted a piece of metal into his cap to protect himself in case a pitcher threw at his head.

That's the way things were in the late 1940s. There is one symbolic moment that captures the time. Pee Wee Reese was a southerner from Louisville, Kentucky. He was the Dodgers shortstop. One day, when fans were giving Jackie a hard time, Reese walked over and put his arm around Jackie. At that moment, the fans stopped

Jackie Robinson was the first Major League Baseball player to appear on a U.S. postage stamp.

Jackie Robinson returns an autograph book to a fan during spring training in 1948.

heckling Jackie. It was a wonderful gesture that showed that Jackie was now part of the team.

In Jackie's first year of Major League Baseball, he helped the Dodgers win the National League pennant. He batted .297, hit 12 home runs, and stole 29 bases. When the season was over, he was voted the National League Rookie of the Year. Two years later, in 1949, he had an amazing year, as he again led the Dodgers to the pennant. This time, he batted .342 and stole 37 bases. Both would be his career highs. He capped off that season by winning the National League's Most Valuable Player award. In three short seasons, Jackie had done more in baseball than just about any other player. It wasn't just the numbers. He proved black men could not only play Major League Baseball, but they could play just as well, if not better, than white men.

In 10 seasons, he compiled a career batting average of .311 and stole 197 bases. He stole home an astounding 19 times. He played in six World Series, the crowning moment coming in 1955 when the Brooklyn Dodgers beat the New York Yankees, winning their first ever world championship. He even stole home in that World Series. But his achievements were much greater than that. Because of the path he blazed, the doors of baseball were swung open to all minority players. Baseball today is multicultural. There are players on the same team from all over the world. And it all started with Jackie. But it was even bigger than that. Many people credit Jackie for helping to integrate America, not just baseball.

Of course, he was voted into the Hall of Fame the first year he was eligible—the first black to be inducted. During his induction speech in 1962, he touched on what he had been through early in his career. He said, "I want to thank all of the people throughout this country who were so wonderful during those trying days." The Hall of Fame was only one of many honors that he received. There are stadiums and schools around the country that are named for Jackie. And maybe the ultimate tribute from baseball is that his No. 42 has been retired not only by the Dodgers but by every team in Major League Baseball. On the 50th anniversary of breaking the color barrier, April 15, 1997, a special ceremony was held at Shea Stadium in New York. President Bill Clinton, Jackie's widow Rachel, Jackie's daughter Sharon, and Branch Rickey III, the grandson of the Dodger president who signed Jackie, were all in attendance.

It's widely believed that Ruth changed baseball but that Jackie changed America. How's that for a legacy? I'd say pretty significant.

Jackie Robinson proudly holds his MVP award.

Jackie thanked three individuals during his Hall of Fame induction speech in 1962:

1. **BRANCH RICKEY:** "A man I considered a father."
2. **HIS MOTHER MALLIE:** "Who taught me so much of the important things early in life."
3. **HIS WIFE RACHEL:** "She's been such a wonderful inspiration to me."

ROGER
BANNISTER

How fast can a man run a mile? In a 26.2-mile marathon, a really great time is around 2 hours and 10 minutes. To accomplish that feat, you'd have to average 5-minute miles, which is pretty amazing. There was a time when 4 minutes and 36.5 seconds for one mile was pretty super. In 1865, an English runner named Richard Webster ran the mile in 4:36.5. It's believed that he held the first "world record" in the mile.

But runners always go faster and faster, and by the year 1900, 21 seconds had been lopped off that "record." But still, the record was 4:15.4—a far cry from 4:00. The runners kept inching closer and closer. And by the year 1945 the world record for the mile stood at 4:01.4. It was held by a Swedish runner named Gunder Hägg. And 4:01.4 is where it stood, just 1.4 seconds away from the magic 4-minute barrier. It would take another nine years before Roger Bannister would run his way into the record books.

Roger had two loves: medicine and running. He won a scholarship to Oxford, where he could do both. Despite his growing fame as a runner, Roger chose not to compete in the 1948 Olympics. He wanted to spend his time studying medicine instead. But Roger decided to make a go of it at the 1952 Olympics in Helsinki, Finland.

Roger wasn't your typical athlete who trained all day. He couldn't because he was studying to become a doctor. That lack of serious training hurt him in the 1952 Olympics. He finished fourth in the 1500 meters. No medal. It was then that Roger decided to dedicate himself to doing the unthinkable: breaking the 4-minute mile.

It happened on his home track at Oxford University. He was now 25 years old. The morning of May 6, 1954, was windy and rainy. Roger was disappointed. He had been aiming for this date to run his way into history. The rain stopped, but the wind continued

Roger Bannister (No. 41) follows Chris Brasher (No. 44) during the first lap of the race on May 6, 1954.

The P.A. announcer at the race, **NORRIS MCWHIRTER**, later created the *Guinness Book of Records*.

train to Oxford for the track meet. I don't know for sure, but I'll bet no other significant sports record was set after an athlete spent part of his day in the library.

The mile-long race was four laps, each one-quarter mile. Roger's strategy was rather simple. He had two buddies in the race: Chris Brasher and Chris Chataway. They would be "rabbits," setting a fast pace for Roger. When the race began, Brasher immediately took the lead. Roger settled into second place and Chataway third. And that's where they stayed for the first lap. To beat 4:00, Roger had to average under 1:00 per lap. And at the quarter-mile mark, he had. Brasher led the way with a time of 57.4 seconds. And they kept the same order for the second quarter mile. Brasher, Roger, Chataway. The second quarter was a little slower. In fact, it was over a minute. But halfway through, the time was 1:58.2.

Now Brasher's work was done, and early in the third lap, Chataway took over the lead. So, now it was Chataway first and Roger second. And when they finished three-quarters of a mile, there was a bit of concern. The time was 3:00.5. Roger knew that to break the record, he would have to run a fabulous last quarter. He'd have to do it in under a minute. Would his quirky training technique pay off? Was running less than an hour a day enough?

to blow. And then, just moments before the race, the wind stopped. The conditions were just right for his record attempt. Less than 3,000 spectators were on hand to witness history. They were mostly Oxford students.

But there were still doubts about whether he could do it. Roger was not training full-time. He would work out maybe 35 minutes a day. That's all. And, of course, there was still his medical career. In fact, the morning of that historic day, he was doing medical research in a London hospital. When he was finished, he took the

With just 250 yards to go, Roger surged to the lead. With long loping strides, he was charging to the finish line. Would he break the barrier that had never been broken? Could a human run a mile in under 4 minutes? He broke the tape and stumbled into the arms of his coach. He was exhausted. He wondered if he had broken the record.

It took a couple of agonizing minutes before the public address announcer Norris McWhirter spoke. And he was dramatic. "Ladies and gentlemen," he began, drawing out his announcement. He mentioned Roger's name, where he was from, and that he had set a track record. He mentioned that the record still had to be made official by the experts. He finally started to mention Roger's time. He said "3." But nobody heard the rest; it was drowned out by the cheering. Roger Bannister had become the first man to smash the 4-minute barrier, with a time of 3:59.4. Roger thanked Brasher and Chataway for setting the pace. He said he was "overwhelmed." And he also admitted that he was lucky that the weather cooperated.

The record didn't last long. Just six weeks. But it didn't matter. Roger was the first. Some compared his achievement to Charles Lindbergh flying solo across the Atlantic Ocean.

But being a record holder, if only for six weeks, was just one of the titles he held. He later became Dr. Roger

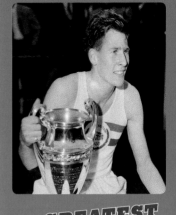

ROGER BANNISTER

BORN: March 23, 1929
BIRTHPLACE: Harrow, Middlesex, England
HEIGHT: 6'2.5"

FAST FACT: Sir Roger Bannister was knighted by Queen Elizabeth II in 1975—not for his running abilities but for his work as a neurologist.

The **GREATEST MOMENTS** *in* **SPORTS**

MILE-LONG MILESTONES

YEAR	RUNNER	TIME
1954	Roger Bannister from England	3:59.4
1967	Jim Ryun from the United States	3:51.1
1999	Hicham El Guerrouj from Morocco	3:43.13

Bannister. Then, it was "Sportsman of the Year" by *Sports Illustrated* magazine. And, finally, he became Sir Roger Bannister, as he was knighted by the Queen of England.

He wanted to be a doctor, not an athlete. And yet, by becoming the first to break one of the most famous sports "barriers," this medical student wound up making history.

BREAKING THE CURSE OF THE BAMBINO

The Boston Red Sox won the 1918 World Series. No big deal. It was their fourth championship in seven years. They had a player named Babe Ruth who not only pitched and won 13 games but also led the American League in home runs with 11 despite only batting part-time. Boston had a dynasty, not to mention the most exciting player in baseball who was a great pitcher *and* a great hitter. In 1919, Boston moved Ruth to the outfield, and it's no surprise that he led the major leagues in home runs and runs batted in. But then came a big surprise: the Red Sox sold him to the Yankees.

How did the sale work out for both teams? Well, the Yankees had never been to the World Series. In Ruth's second season, the Yanks made it to the Fall Classic. His third and fourth seasons too. In 1923, the Yankees won their first World Series, and they kept on winning them. Over the next 80 years, the Yanks won 26 World Series titles. As for the Red Sox? They won exactly none. Zero. Zip. Over time, they started to call it the "Curse of the Bambino." As you know, "Bambino" was one of Ruth's nicknames. Boston was somehow cursed because they sold Ruth to the Yankees. As you can imagine, Red Sox fans developed a real dislike for the rival Yankees.

Was it really a curse? It sure seemed that way. After Ruth left, the Red Sox didn't get back to the World Series until 1946. They lost to St. Louis in seven games. They made it to another World Series in 1967—same teams, same result. In 1975, they battled Cincinnati in the World Series. And again they lost in Game 7. In 1978, the Red Sox faced the Yankees in a one-game playoff. The winner would go to the World Series. Of course, Boston lost 5–4. Next up was a heartbreaking seventh-game loss to the New York

BOSTON'S
WORLD SERIES
WINS AND LOSSES

2007	**4–0**	**BOSTON RED SOX VS. COLORADO ROCKIES**
2004	**4–0**	**BOSTON RED SOX VS. ST. LOUIS CARDINALS**
1986	4–3	NEW YORK METS VS. BOSTON RED SOX
1975	4–3	CINCINNATI REDS VS. BOSTON RED SOX
1967	4–3	ST. LOUIS CARDINALS VS. BOSTON RED SOX
1946	4–3	ST. LOUIS CARDINALS VS. BOSTON RED SOX
1918	**4–2**	**BOSTON RED SOX VS. CHICAGO CUBS**
1916	**4–1**	**BOSTON RED SOX VS. BROOKLYN ROBINS**
1915	**4–1**	**BOSTON RED SOX VS. PHILADELPHIA PHILLIES**
1912	**4–3–1**	**BOSTON RED SOX VS. NEW YORK GIANTS**
1903	**5–3**	**BOSTON AMERICANS VS. PITTSBURGH PIRATES**

(Note: Boston's winning years are in bold.)

Babe Ruth's last season in a Red Sox uniform was 1919.

Mets in 1986. Boston's totals were four World Series, four losses, all in the seventh game.

Yup, it seemed like they were cursed for sure.

The century came to a close with the 1999 playoffs. And wouldn't you know it, the Red Sox faced the Yankees for the American League pennant. The Yankees easily won in five games before clinching yet another World Series. The Red Sox went home empty-handed, as they had done every year since 1918.

Would the new century reverse the curse? It didn't look that way. In 2003, Boston again faced New York for the American League pennant. The series was tied three games apiece. Just one more win, and the Red Sox would finally beat the hated Yankees. Game 7 was

Fenway Park is famous for the big green wall in left field known as the "Green Monster."

played at Yankee Stadium in New York. And with their best pitcher on the mound, Pedro Martinez, the Red Sox raced out to a 4–0 lead in the fourth inning. But as you've probably guessed, they didn't hold on, and the Yankees went on to another World Series. The Red Sox were going home again, unquestionably cursed.

Things didn't seem any better in 2004. The Red Sox and Yankees met again for the American League pennant, and the Yankees were rolling. They won the first three games. The third game was a disaster for the Red Sox. The Yankees won the game in Fenway Park 19–8. They weren't only beating the Red Sox they were humiliating them. No team in baseball history had ever come

Boston's David Ortiz rounds first base after hitting the game-winning home run in Game 4 against the Yankees.

Curt Schilling pitches the Red Sox to victory despite a serious ankle injury.

Boston's outfielder, MANNY RAMIREZ, received the World Series MVP award in 2004.

back from losing the first three games to win a series. Boston certainly wouldn't do it. Not with the "Curse of the Bambino."

The Yankees went for the sweep in Game 4. They led 4–3 going into the bottom of the ninth inning. And they had their dominant relief pitcher, Mariano Rivera, on the mound. Just three more outs, and Boston would be finished again—as usual. But something amazing happened. The Red Sox scored a run in the bottom of the ninth to tie the score. And in the bottom of the twelfth inning, David Ortiz hit a two-run homer to win the game. Boston had finally won. But they still trailed three games to one in the series.

The next night, the same thing happened. Boston rallied late to tie the game, and Ortiz had the game-winning single in the fourteenth inning. The Red Sox were still alive! But now the series shifted back to Yankee Stadium for Game 6. Curt Schilling was the Boston pitcher.

He had an ankle injury that wasn't completely healed. In fact, as he pitched, you could see blood on his sock. Yet, Schilling pitched the Red Sox to victory. They had miraculously won three games in a row to tie the series. But could they do the impossible and win four straight?

Game 7 started with a bang. Ortiz smashed a two-run homer in the top of the first. The next inning, Johnny Damon hit a grand slam for the Red Sox. It was 6–0 Boston, and they cruised to a 10–3 win. They had finally vanquished the Yankees. But did that end the curse? Some argued that unless Boston won the World Series, the curse would not be broken.

The Red Sox took care of that in a hurry. They swept the St. Louis Cardinals in four straight games. Newspapers in Boston blared the headlines: "Yes!!!" "Finally!" "Amen!" All of New England rejoiced as the Red Sox had won their first World Series in 86 years.

David Ortiz hits a home run during the World Series.

And now, at long last, they were champions of the world. During the playoffs, Damon came up with a nickname. The players called themselves "idiots." They had a carefree attitude and they didn't believe in the "Curse of the Bambino." After the World Series, they held a parade in Boston for the Red Sox. Around three million people showed up to salute the champions. Generation after generation of Red Sox fans had known nothing but disappointment.

But now, what curse? It was an "idiots' delight."

THE
IMMACULATE
RECEPTION

Quick—name the greatest franchise in NFL history. You might answer the Pittsburgh Steelers. After all, they've won more Super Bowls than any other team. But if you think that the Boston Red Sox had some bad years, wait until you hear about the Steelers. The Steelers were founded in 1933, and they were awful. For example, in 1939 and 1941, they had just one win the entire season. They did even worse in 1944. No wins, 0 and 10. They finally made it to the playoffs in 1947. They lost to Philadelphia 21–0. And that was their entire playoff history until the 1970s. Nobody was worse.

But in football, there is an upside to being bad. The worse you are, the better you draft. And in 1969, when Pittsburgh finished a miserable 1 and 13, it meant they owned the first draft pick in 1970. With the number one pick, they chose a quarterback from Louisiana Tech named Terry Bradshaw. It was the beginning of the turnaround. Two seasons later, with the 13th pick, they chose a running back named Franco Harris from Penn State. Bradshaw and Harris combined for one of the most astounding plays in the history of sports.

The date was December 23, 1972, at Three Rivers Stadium in Pittsburgh. The Steelers were hosting the Oakland Raiders in an AFC playoff game. Unlike Pittsburgh, Oakland had a winning history. They had already played in a Super Bowl, and even though they didn't come into existence until 1960, by 1972, they had appeared in eight playoff games. The Pittsburgh Steelers had been in existence for four decades, and this was just their second playoff game in franchise history.

The game was low scoring. In fact, Pittsburgh was leading 6–0 until just 1:13 remained in the game. Oakland's talented quarterback Ken Stabler, known as "the Snake," was an effective runner. He took the ball and ran it 30 yards for a touchdown. The Raiders had

MEMBERS OF THE 1972 STEELERS IN THE PRO FOOTBALL HALL OF FAME

PLAYER	POSITION
Mel Blount	Cornerback
Terry Bradshaw	Quarterback
"Mean" Joe Greene	Defensive Tackle
Jack Ham	Linebacker
Franco Harris	Running Back
Chuck Noll	Coach
Art Rooney	Owner

Franco Harris, the running back for the Pittsburgh Steelers.

taken the lead 7–6. Surely Pittsburgh would lose again. History told us so. They had never won a playoff game, and on this day, they hadn't even scored a touchdown. What happened next was the stuff of legend.

It all came down to one final play for Pittsburgh. They faced a fourth down and 10 from their own 40-yard line with just 22 seconds left in the game. The entire season was on the line. Bradshaw took the snap and dropped back to pass. He faced a ferocious pass rush from the Raiders defense. He escaped one tackle and then another. And then he fired the ball downfield to about the 35-yard line of Oakland. If you were watching on television that day, as I was, you saw the ball bounce into the air. You figured it was an incomplete pass. But moments later, the camera caught the rookie Harris running with the ball. He was charging down the left sideline and into the end zone for a touchdown. The Steelers had won the game. Or had they? How did Harris get the ball? And most important, was it a legal play?

Here's what happened. Bradshaw's pass was intended for Frenchy Fuqua, a Steelers running back. Just as the ball arrived, the Raiders bruising defensive back, Jack Tatum, smashed into Fuqua. What the TV camera didn't catch at first was that the ball popped into the air and just before it hit the ground, Harris, who was trailing the play, reached down and scooped the ball out of the air. But again, was it legal? At the time, there was a rule that said two offensive players couldn't touch a pass in succession. If the ball had hit off Fuqua and was then caught by Harris, under NFL rules at the time, it would have been an illegal forward pass and the Raiders would have won the game.

The officials huddled up. Pittsburgh claimed it was a touchdown. The Raiders argued it wasn't. There was no instant replay in use back then. Then, the decision came. The refs ruled that the ball bounced off Tatum of Oakland, not Fuqua of Pittsburgh.

Franco Harris (No. 32) runs from Jimmy Ware of the Oakland Raiders and scores the winning touchdown.

LISTEN to this MOMENT TRACK 10

It was a touchdown! The Pittsburgh Steelers had won their first-ever playoff game on one of the wackiest plays in football history.

It seemed that the Pittsburgh franchise turned around on that one crazy play. No, they didn't win the NFL championship that year—the undefeated Miami Dolphins did. But that was the beginning of the Steelers dynasty. Before the 1970s were over, the Steelers had won four Super Bowls. They won a fifth after the 2005 season and a record-setting sixth in Super Bowl XLIII in 2009. After 40 years of futility, the Pittsburgh Steelers were now viewed as the most successful team in the NFL.

As for that rule about two offensive players touching the ball consecutively on the same pass play? That was later changed. And, as you know, instant replay also came into football. But what about those players? Bradshaw and Harris both wound up in the Pro Football Hall of Fame. Tatum swore forever that he never touched the ball and that the play should have been ruled illegal.

There's a statue in a Pittsburgh museum that depicts Harris reaching down and scooping the ball out of mid-air. It forever memorializes that split second in time. It was just an amazing moment and one of the greatest in the history of sports.

THE MIRACLE ON ICE

The moments in this book display either great individual or team accomplishment, often overcoming long odds. The results are either unexpected or of such magnitude that everyone had to stand up and take notice. But no sports event gripped the country like the 1980 Winter Olympics in Lake Placid, New York. Specifically, the hockey team.

In those days, professional players weren't permitted in the Olympics, only unpaid amateurs. In the United States, the country's best players were a part of the National Hockey League. But those players weren't allowed in the Olympics because they were paid athletes. Countries like the Soviet Union didn't have a National Hockey League, so the best hockey players were on their country's Olympic team.

The United States and the Soviet Union were the two major world powers in 1980, and they were major rivals. So, when the Olympics came around every four years, in the eyes of most Americans, it was "the good guys vs. the bad guys." And the Soviets usually won. They won the gold medal in hockey in the last four Olympic Games before 1980. They were virtually unbeatable. In fact, the U.S. hockey team played the Soviets at Madison Square Garden in New York City the week before the Lake Placid Olympics. The Soviets trounced the Americans 10–3. Many people wondered: Why should the U.S. hockey team bother going to the Olympics? Maybe they should just give the Soviets another gold medal and not waste everyone's time.

The Soviet team had some grizzled veterans of international hockey. Their goaltender was the great Vladislav Tretiak. He was 27 years old. Their terrific left winger, Valeri Kharlamov, was 32. However, the United States had a bunch of young college kids on the 1980 Olympic hockey team. The captain of the U.S. team was left winger Mike Eruzione from Boston University. He was the oldest man on the team at 25 years old.

The goaltender, Jim Craig, Eruzione's teammate from Boston University, was only 22. Many of the American players were even younger than that.

The U.S. team was coached by Herb Brooks, the University of Minnesota hockey coach. He was a disciplinarian who knew all about heartbreak. He was the last player cut from the 1960 U.S. Olympic hockey team. That team went on without him to win the gold medal in Squaw Valley, California.

Coach Brooks was a hard taskmaster. He emphasized teamwork and skating. Once, when the United States played against Norway in an exhibition game in Oslo before the Olympics, the game ended in a tie. Brooks wasn't happy with his team's effort. So, after the game, after all the fans had gone home, with the lights of the arena turned off, he dragged his team back onto the ice and made them skate until they dropped. The drills were known as "Herbies." Players had to skate as fast as they could and then stop. Then start again. Then stop. And that night in Oslo, they did it in the dark, over and over and over again. That's the kind of disciplinarian Brooks was.

The first game the U.S. team played in the 1980 Olympics was against Sweden. The United States trailed in the third period. Turns out, they would trail in virtually every game they played. It took a goal by Bill Baker with just 27 seconds remaining to escape with a 2–2 tie. Next up was Czechoslovakia. The Czechs were expecting to contend for the silver medal. But the American kids stunned them by winning the game 7–3. And talk about teamwork. The seven goals were scored by seven different players!

Norway was next. Remember the tie game that got the coach so angry? Not this time. The surprising U.S. team won 5–1. And they didn't stop. They played Romania, and it was another big win, 7–2. And then, they played West Germany. The Germans went up 2–0. But in a stirring comeback, the United States won the game 4–2. The Americans had played five games. They had four wins and a tie. Next up—the medal round and a date with the mighty Soviets.

It was Friday, February 22, 1980. It was the most anticipated hockey game in U.S. history—and not just among sports fans. All Americans wanted to see if this group of kids could do the unthinkable and beat the mighty Soviets. The Soviet team had not lost an Olympic hockey game since 1968, a stretch of 21 games. They had not lost the Olympic gold medal since 1960. And remember the thrashing they gave the United States at Madison Square Garden? They were the overwhelming favorites to put the Americans in their place. Before the game began, Coach Brooks had a simple message for his team: "You're meant to be here. This moment is yours."

And then the game began. It was a boisterous crowd at Lake Placid. They were waving American flags and chanting "U-S-A, U-S-A." It was a back-and-forth first period. The Soviets scored first and then the Americans tied it. The Soviets regained the lead and then one of the biggest moments of the tournament occurred. Trailing 2–1 in the final seconds of the first period, a couple of kids from Minnesota combined to tie the game. Dave Christian took a long shot that was stopped by the Soviet goaltender Tretiak. Mark Johnson was there for the rebound, and he scored to tie the game with no time remaining on the clock. They went to their locker rooms tied at 2.

The Soviet coach then pulled a surprising move. He replaced his goaltender. Backup Vladimir Myshkin took over for the great Tretiak. Even the players were surprised. But it seemed to work. The United States didn't score a goal in the second period. The Soviets took the lead. It could have been worse for the Americans, but

Craig was fabulous, turning away shot after shot. With one period remaining, the Soviets led the game 3–2.

The third period began, and the Americans tied the game on another goal from Johnson. It was now 3–3 with just 10 minutes to go. And then it happened. The captain, Eruzione,

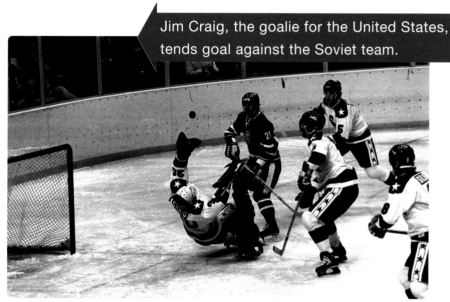

Jim Craig, the goalie for the United States, tends goal against the Soviet team.

Jim Craig deflects a puck shot by Helmut Balderis (No. 19) from the Soviet team.

about to happen. On television, the announcer calling the game for ABC, Al Michaels, yelled out: "Do you believe in miracles? Yes!"

LISTEN *to this* **MOMENT** **TRACK 11**

They had done it. A group of college kids from America had defeated the mighty, unbeatable Soviets 4–3. The players mobbed each other while the flag-waving crowd cheered at the top of their lungs. But there was still another game to play.

The United States had to play Finland two days later with the gold medal on the line. Just one game to go.

As usual, the United States fell behind. But trailing 2–1 in the third period, they scored three straight goals to beat Finland 4–2 and capture the gold medal. For the medal ceremony, there was room on the podium for just the team captain. But when Eruzione went up to receive his gold medal, he motioned for all his teammates to come up with him. How fitting. This was truly a team effort. All that hard work and all those "Herbies" had paid off. And in many ways it was a national victory. Americans everywhere felt enormous pride in what these kids had done. They had boosted the spirits of an entire country. It was truly a "Miracle on Ice" and, in my opinion, the greatest moment in American sports history.

LIFE AFTER THE OLYMPICS

JIM CRAIG played in 30 NHL games, 23 of them with Boston.

MIKE ERUZIONE didn't play a single NHL game.

the old man on the team, fired a shot that went in! The arena went crazy. The Americans had taken their first lead of the game, 4–3. But there were still 10 long minutes to go.

The great Soviets were not about to give up. Neither was Craig. He stopped every shot the Soviets took. They took 39 shots during the entire game, and Craig stopped 36 of them. By contrast, the Americans only had 16 shots on goal, but they made theirs count. As the final seconds ticked off the clock, the arena was in a frenzy. The impossible was

POSTSCRIPT

So, there you have it. My vote for the Greatest Moments in Sports. Now it's your turn. Go to LenBerman Sports.com and vote for your greatest sports moments. Hopefully, they were in this book. If not, your vote still counts. We're collecting ideas for another book, and who knows—maybe you'll be the one who comes up with a great moment that makes the list. In the meantime, I hope you keep watching sports. You never know when one of the greatest moments in sports history will occur. It could happen right before your very eyes!

ABOUT THE AUTHOR

Photo Courtesy: Norman/Marquee Photography

Len Berman has been a sportscaster for over 40 years. He has covered just about every major sports event, including multiple Super Bowls, World Series, and Olympics. He is the creator of "Spanning the World," a monthly collection of sports bloopers that's been a 20-year staple on NBC's *Today Show*. He is also the creator of *Sports Fantasy*, which aired on NBC in the 1980s, pitting regular viewers against famous sports stars. He is the recipient of eight Emmy Awards. This is his fourth book.

A native New Yorker, Len graduated from Syracuse University and resides on Long Island with his wife, Jill. They have three children.

AUDIO CREDITS:

Len Berman was recorded by Dubway Studios, New York, New York. Audio production engineering by Stephen Schappler.

Some audio segments have been edited for time and content. Some archival audio quality is the result of source limitations. Archival audio copyright and used with permission of:

ABC Sports, Inc.	Fox Sports, Inc.	NBA Entertainment, Inc.
CBS Sports, Inc.	NBC Sports, Inc.	NFL Films, Inc.
ESPN Enterprises, Inc.	Major League Baseball Properties, Inc.	New York Racing Association

Special thanks to the amazing broadcasters who brought to life the great moments on our CD:

Troy Aikman	Bill Campbell	Milo Hamilton	Jim Simpson
Chick Anderson	Bob Costas	Al Michaels	Joe Starkey
Joe Buck	Curt Gowdy	Bob Miller	